Claim Your Fre

www.questionsaboutme.co

CW00556685

Like our Facebook page
@QuestionsAboutMe

Follow us on Instagram
@QuestionsAboutMe_Official

Questions & Customer Service
hello@questionsaboutme.com

2000 Would You Rather Questions About Me

by Questions About Me™

www.questionsaboutme.com

Introduction

Communication is key for meaningful relationships, but we often rely on small talk and dull exchanges without truly engaging others in deep conversation.

2000 Would You Rather Questions About Me is a tool to help spark engaging discussions and thoughts. You can use *2000 Would You Rather Questions About Me* to unlock endless conversational possibilities with someone you've known for years or someone you've recently met.

Enjoy learning more about yourself and foster conversation and engagement with others.

Ask yourself these dilemma-style questions or use them as conversation prompts with family and friends—even strangers!—to cultivate meaningful and fun discussions. These thought-provoking dilemmas will help you communicate and connect in an easy and entertaining way.

We've intentionally made the questions random so they're spontaneous. The dilemmas have been created for adults, but they're suitable for children as young as nine years old—we've included some extra easy questions for younger audiences.

Our *Questions About Me* series is for everyone—there's no adult content and the questions are free from political affiliation and religious preference.

How to Use this Book

» You must choose an answer! The dilemmas will make you think and force you to make a choice.

» Going deeper with your answers by explaining your logic will lead to rewarding explorations and discussions.

» Don't be afraid to go off-topic. The wide range of intriguing scenarios will result in interesting conversations, lively discussions, and endless laughs!

» The format of this book is flexible and the questions can be tackled any way you like. You can skip around and answer questions, or you can start at the beginning and work through them in order.

» The writing space is purposely limited so you can use this book as a tool in a variety of ways—ask the questions out loud, fill in your responses, or answer the questions in your journal.

» Put down your phone, switch off the TV, and declare the time you spend answering these questions a no-judgment zone.

» Remember, there are no correct or incorrect answers. Allow yourself to be vulnerable and don't hold back with your responses.

You can enjoy our *Questions About Me* series on your own, one-on-one, or in a group setting.

Yourself

- » Use as a guided journal, or question-a-day journal, for writing prompts or for creative inspiration.
- » Complete the questions as a mindfulness activity for self-reflection, personal growth, and better self-understanding.
- » Give a completed book to someone special as a keepsake.
- » Offer it as a unique and thoughtful gift to friends, family, a significant other, or yourself.

One-on-one

- » Take turns asking questions with your significant other. Strengthen your relationship and bond with your partner by learning more about each other. (You could also get your partner to answer the questions as if they were you.)
- » Deepen your knowledge of those closest to you. Discover new things information about your kids, parents, siblings, and close friends with questions you never thought to ask.

Group discussions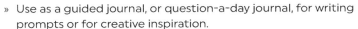

- » Stir up fun conversations at gatherings with family or friends at the dinner table, family events, or as a holiday activity.
- » Download the book and use while traveling.
- » Level up your conversation skills at networking events, team-building games, business trips, ice-breaker activities, job interviews, or therapy sessions.

The most important thing to know about using this book is: **There is no wrong way to use this book.** What's important is that you have fun.

No matter how you choose to use this book, enjoy using our *Questions About Me* series in any context or social situation to ignite meaningful connections and conversations.

01   WYR lose an arm or a leg?

02   WYR be too hot or too cold?

03   WYR live in a world where nothing is square or one where nothing is round?

04   WYR be caught in an earthquake or a tornado?

05   WYR give up chocolate or cheese?

06   WYR be the size of a giraffe or the size of an ant for the day?

07   WYR hang out with King Arthur or Robin Hood?

08   WYR have a tree house or an underground bunker?

09   WYR eat your least favorite food once a week or eat your favorite food only once a week?

10   WYR be able to swim like a fish or climb like a gecko?

11   WYR all your clothes had to be fastened with buttons or with zippers?

12   WYR reduce or recycle?

13   WYR have hiccups or a persistent cough for the day?

14   WYR be a world-class tap dancer or a world-class line dancer?

15   WYR take the stairs or use the elevator?

16   WYR cook a meal for six or wash the dishes after a meal for six?

17   WYR wear all stripes or all spots?

18   WYR shave off your hair or shave off your eyebrows?

19   WYR never eat red-colored food or never eat green-colored food again?

20   WYR never cut your fingernails or never cut your toenails again?

21   WYR be allergic to cola or coffee?

22   WYR receive $100 per day for life or receive one lump sum of $1 million?

23   WYR play a game of Scrabble or a game of Twister?

24   WYR have fur or feathers?

25   WYR visit the moon or the bottom of the deepest ocean?

26   WYR always be twenty minutes early or always be ten minutes late?

27   WYR have the go-ahead to get to the front of any line or always have traffic lights go green as you approach?

28   WYR sit in the very front row or the very back row in a cinema?

29   WYR be a boy named Sue or a girl named Hank?

30   WYR know everything there is to know or have access to the resources to research everything?

31   WYR have one lifelong friend or lots of short-term friends?

32   WYR have tea with Sir Richard Branson or Sir David Attenborough?

33   WYR find the key to a secret door or the key to a secret box?

34   WYR have a grandfather clock or a cuckoo clock?

35   WYR do a sponsored parachute jump or a sponsored bungee jump?

36   WYR come face to face with a vampire or a werewolf?

37   WYR colonize the moon or Mars?

38   WYR there were only cats or only dogs in the world?

39   WYR never wear shoes or never go barefoot?

40   WYR know how to hunt or know how to fish?

41   WYR have an attic or a basement in your home?

42   WYR have an open-plan living space or separate rooms in your home?

43   WYR bring a T-Rex or a woolly mammoth back to life?

44 WYR slur your words like you're drunk or only be able to speak like a baby?

45 WYR dress like a Roman soldier or talk like a pirate for a month?

46 WYR forget how to read or forget how to write?

47 WYR float like a butterfly or sting like a bee?

48 WYR have no heating or no air conditioning?

49 WYR end world poverty or find a cure for cancer?

50 WYR be fluent in three languages or be able to talk to animals?

51 WYR be somewhere over the rainbow or somewhere down the crazy river?

52 WYR have hooves or claws?

53 WYR be a fly on the wall or a snake in the grass?

54 WYR visit Middle-earth or Narnia?

55 WYR be a cyclops or a three-eyed monster?

56 WYR have your hands double in size or your feet double in size?

57 WYR burn your finger or your tongue?

58 WYR be a solid-rooted tree or a leaf in the breeze?

59 WYR have the speed of a cheetah or the strength of a gorilla?

60 WYR be a champion cheerleader for a team you don't like or a mediocre cheerleader for a team you love?

61 WYR take a risk or play it safe?

62 WYR survive a plane crash into a jungle or into a desert?

63 WYR have no hot water in your home or no indoor toilet?

64 WYR love your job and get paid a little or hate your job and get paid a lot?

65 WYR be attacked by two angry geese or six angry Chihuahuas?

66 WYR be able to make your own clothes or grow your own food?

67 WYR never see the sea again or never see green fields again?

68 WYR have to sing everything you say or repeat everything you say?

69 WYR wear your slippers to work or your work shoes to the beach?

70 WYR do a thousand-piece jigsaw wearing ski gloves or walk up ten flights of stairs wearing scuba diving fins?

71 WYR be able to breathe underwater or see in the dark?

72 WYR save the last tree on Earth or the last bee on Earth?

73 WYR never have another cold or never have to charge up your devices?

74 WYR be the boss or be the boss's chief advisor?

75 WYR the last page of your book was missing or the last five minutes of the movie you're watching?

76 WYR not be able to read the labels in a supermarket or not be able to read the menu in a restaurant?

77 WYR be invisible or be able to read minds?

78 WYR have only touchscreen devices or only keyboard devices?

79 WYR have a beak for a week or walk on all-fours for a week?

80 WYR only be able to read books for the rest of your life or only be able to watch movies for the rest of your life?

81 WYR be the best musician in a little-known band or the weakest musician in a well-known band?

82 WYR have a celebrity chef for a week or a housekeeper for a month?

83 WYR circumnavigate the globe as a solo yachtsperson or in a hot air balloon?

84 WYR have a huge surprise party organized in your honor or have an unlimited budget to organize a party for someone else?

85 WYR win the Nobel Prize for Medicine or for Peace?

86   WYR have permanent dandruff or a constantly runny nose?

87   WYR be as sly as a fox or as gentle as a lamb?

88   WYR a professional photographer took your picture or a professional stylist styled your hair?

89   WYR never have to work again or never have to pay bills again?

90   WYR play hide and seek in the dark or dodgeball in the dark?

91   WYR have the eye of the tiger or eyes like a hawk?

92   WYR accidentally brush your teeth with soap or wash your hair with toilet cleaner?

93   WYR your eyes could see like a microscope or far into the distance like binoculars?

94   WYR go out in public wearing just your oldest, ugliest underwear or just fig leaves?

95   WYR be on a glass-bottomed boat or in a glass-roofed submarine?

96   WYR lose the money you made this year or the memories you made this year?

97   WYR have hiccups or a persistent cough for the day?

98   WYR be put on a puréed food diet or a raw food diet?

99   WYR give up all the money you earn in the next five years or give up the savings you have now?

100   WYR be hypnotized to dance every time you said "yes" or sing every time you said "no"?

101   WYR have ninja-like stealth or gladiator-like strength?

102   WYR eat dinner alone for a year or eat with a group of people you don't like for a year?

103   WYR bring back Elvis or Princess Diana?

104   WYR have no washing machine or no shower in your home for a year?

105 WYR be able to press a fast-forward button or a rewind button in your life?

106 WYR only have access to YouTube or only have access to games on your device?

107 WYR be the first or the last to know the world is ending?

108 WYR crawl 200 yards across a floor of mousetraps or swim 200 yards through shark-infested waters?

109 WYR your face aged ten years overnight or your body from the neck down aged fifteen years overnight?

110 WYR win $10,000 or have your friend win $25,000?

111 WYR have someone constantly finish your sentences or someone constantly interrupt your conversations?

112 WYR an alarm sounded every time you said a curse word or every time you lied?

113 WYR be able to run but have nowhere to hide or hide and have nowhere to run?

114 WYR win an all-expenses-paid dream vacation or go on tour with your favorite band?

115 WYR have your toes stepped on every day or your hair pulled every day?

116 WYR be trapped in a small space with 5,000 locusts for ten minutes or eat ten locusts in five minutes?

117 WYR never be able to wear the latest fashion or never be able to change your hairstyle?

118 WYR always have an itchy nose or have at least one pimple on your face?

119 WYR have one job for the rest of your life or change jobs every two years?

120 WYR become half-human, half-fly or half-human, half-spider?

121 WYR be able to play every musical instrument or sing every song?

122 WYR split your pants in public or snort out a booger when you laugh in public?

123 WYR be a secret benefactor or a famous philanthropist?

124 WYR have a small pebble in your shoe or a dull ringing in your ears?

125 WYR wear shoes that turned you into the greater dancer or shoes that gave you super running speed?

126 WYR collect something few people care about or be an expert in something few people want to know?

127 WYR dress like your parents or only watch the TV shows your parents watch?

128 WYR find a fly in your soup or a worm in your apple?

129 WYR be accused of something you didn't do or have someone else take the credit for something you did do?

130 WYR be stuck in an elevator with a bragger or a moaner?

131 WYR be able to do only one magical spell well or do lots of spells with only a fifty percent chance of success?

132 WYR never sunbathe again or never sit by an open fire again?

133 WYR be mentored by Bill Gates or Oprah Winfrey?

134 WYR be known for being kind or for being someone no one should mess with?

135 WYR be jilted at the altar or be divorced?

136 WYR have been born a decade earlier or a decade later than you were?

137 WYR never get another haircut or get a different trainee stylist every time you get a haircut?

138 WYR wear dark glasses at night or be forbidden from leaving your house after dark?

139 WYR be a fearless adventurer or a mathematical genius?

140 WYR have crackers without cheese or cheese without pickles?

141   WYR be able to walk through walls or see through walls?

142   WYR capsize your canoe into piranha-filled water or parachute into hippo territory?

143   WYR only be able to travel on horseback or by rickshaw?

144   WYR squeeze someone else's pimple or have someone squeeze your pimple?

145   WYR have the cleanliness of your fridge or your oven inspected right now?

146   WYR wake up in the body of a famous historical figure or the body of a reality-TV celebrity?

147   WYR lose three teeth or lose internet connection for three months?

148   WYR wear wet socks every day for a month or wear mitts on your hands every day for a week?

149   WYR be rich with a low IQ or poor with a high IQ?

150   WYR be transported into *Super Mario World* or into a *Candy Crush* world?

151   WYR play checkers or chess?

152   WYR everyone laughed when you walk into a room or everyone cried?

153   WYR tell the truth, no matter what, or tell a lie to save a friend?

154   WYR have someone massage your feet every day or have someone cook a meal for you once a week?

155   WYR emigrate and never return to your homeland or never leave your homeland at all?

156   WYR yawn uncontrollably or have your feet tap uncontrollably every time you hear music?

157   WYR be remembered as a great prankster or a great team player in your schooldays?

158   WYR wake up with a face like a fish or a neck like a giraffe?

159 WYR someone you just met told you your fly was undone or a colleague told you that you have bad breath?

160 WYR have vampire-like fangs or werewolf-like eyes?

161 WYR be telepathic or have the power to heal with your hands?

162 WYR experience zero gravity or be able to dance on the ceiling?

163 WYR spend a day in an enchanted forest or in a magical undersea world?

164 WYR eat in the Great Hall at Hogwarts or feast in Neverland with the Lost Boys?

165 WYR have ears bigger than your hands or arms longer than your legs?

166 WYR bring back an outdated fashion or a forgotten food from decades ago?

167 WYR make snap decisions using your heart or your head?

168 WYR walk the plank or be marooned on a desert island?

169 WYR be stuck in a *Groundhog Day* loop on your first day at work or on a first date?

170 WYR sing a duet with Frank Sinatra or do a dance routine with Laurel and Hardy?

171 WYR visit the Simpsons or the Addams Family?

172 WYR be a guest at a party without food or a party without music?

173 WYR have a secret admirer or secretly know the identity of your secret admirer?

174 WYR eat ten bananas every day or slip on a banana peel every day?

175 WYR survive for a week on dog food or a week on food thrown out by grocery stores?

176 WYR be raised by wolves or monkeys?

177 WYR have your arm in plaster for six weeks or be on a strict liquid-only diet for three weeks?

178 WYR be a robot that builds cars or a robot that performs surgical procedures?

179 WYR have been the first person to walk on the moon or be the first person to walk on Mars?

180 WYR be the captain of a cruise ship or the pilot of a jumbo jet?

181 WYR spend a day on the Starship Enterprise or the Millennium Falcon?

182 WYR be the bearer of bad news or receive bad news?

183 WYR be a world-renowned concert pianist or the keyboard player in a popular tribute band?

184 WYR meet a wolf dressed in sheep's clothing or have the wool pulled over your eyes?

185 WYR be the eighth dwarf in *Snow White* or the fourth member of Alvin and the Chipmunks?

186 WYR be known as a lone wolf or a crowd-pleaser?

187 WYR have six-pack abs or get a free six-pack of potato chips whenever you want one?

188 WYR sneeze six times on the hour every hour or wink six times on the hour?

189 WYR eat a whole jar of mayonnaise straight from the jar or drink one liter of beetroot juice in one sitting?

190 WYR be a wildflower in a woodland or a rare orchid in a pot?

191 WYR be stranded on a desert island with an optimistic self-help guru or a pessimistic doom merchant?

192 WYR have no sense of smell or smell the opposite of what everyone else smells?

193 WYR save the life of one distant relative or save the lives of five people you don't know?

194 WYR survive on uncooked pasta or raw eggs?

195 WYR be a party balloon or a party popper?

196 WYR be locked in a room with no source of light or locked in room with a bright light permanently on?

197 WYR be a box of firecrackers or a supercharged single firework?

198 WYR be once bitten, twice shy or be in for a penny, in for a pound?

199 WYR follow the way of the dragon or follow the yellow brick road?

200 WYR lose weight by sticking to the cabbage soup diet or by doing two high-intensity exercise sessions per day?

201 WYR be caught on CCTV scratching your butt or practicing your dance moves?

202 WYR get to work (school) on stilts or go shopping on the weekend on a hoppity hop?

203 WYR be able to clear traffic jams by clapping your hands or get instant takeout by snapping your fingers?

204 WYR be trapped in a romantic comedy with your enemies or trapped in a horror movie with your friends?

205 WYR have feet like a Hobbit or ears like Dobby the house-elf?

206 WYR sit in a bath of cold baked beans or get or get slimed for charity?

207 WYR be a soccer player's sock or a ski-jumper's glove?

208 WYR see the sun rise from Mount Fuji or see the sun go down in the Serengeti?

209 WYR fail your driving test six times or get dumped six times in a row?

210 WYR be able to swing through trees like Tarzan or talk to animals like Dr. Dolittle?

211 WYR be homeless or live alone with no family and friends?

212 WYR be able to walk on water or have diamonds on the soles of your shoes?

213 WYR die of starvation or sell one of your kidneys to buy food?

214 WYR be reincarnated as a beautiful butterfly with a short life or a stray dog living on the street?

215 WYR be a notorious baddie everyone loves to hate or an unsung hero?

216 WYR have no wrists or no ankles?

217 WYR eat only your favorite meal for every meal or never eat your favorite meal again?

218 WYR wear clown shoes for a day or a clown wig and nose for three days?

219 WYR have only virtual-world video game adventures or have only real-world outdoor adventures?

220 WYR go on a cross-country road trip or a cross-country train trip?

221 WYR spend a weekend in a relaxing spa retreat or in Las Vegas?

222 WYR be a famous athlete or a famous actor playing the role of a famous athlete in a movie?

223 WYR be an early riser or a night owl?

224 WYR only ever hang out with no more than five friends or only ever go to huge parties?

225 WYR be known as witty or wise?

226 WYR live in a world where you never had to work again or one where you never had to sleep again?

227 WYR be afraid of the dark or sunlight?

228 WYR be a deep-sea diver or a high diver?

229 WYR wear dirty clothes or torn clothes?

230 WYR receive $1,000 for kissing a stranger or $1 every time someone kisses you?

231 WYR go wilderness camping off the beaten track or go glamping in a popular tourist spot?

232 WYR your friends described you as someone who eats a lot or someone who sleeps a lot?

233 WYR always eat indoors or always eat outdoors?

234 WYR be an ordinary citizen in a utopian world or be a powerful leader in a dystopian world?

235 WYR be described as stern and stoic or frivolous and fun?

236 WYR be in a dull, long-lasting relationship or an exciting, short-lived relationship?

237 WYR wake up with teeth like a beaver or eyes like a lizard?

238 WYR be Goldilocks or Jiminy Cricket?

239 WYR be the runt of the litter or the black sheep of the family?

240 WYR survive by drinking the water in the toilet brush holder or eating frog spawn?

241 WYR never eat out or eat out once a week at a five-star restaurant for free with someone you don't like?

242 WYR relax by having a massage or by reading a magazine?

243 WYR that oranges were the only fruit you could eat or carrots were the only vegetable you could eat?

244 WYR be like someone else or stay as you are?

245 WYR win the lottery or have everyone in your family (including you) live twice as long?

246 WYR be stranded for an hour on a broken ski lift or a broken rollercoaster?

247 WYR end all war or find a cure for all disease?

248 WYR work your way from rags to riches or win the lottery?

249 WYR be an only child or the youngest of seven children?

250 WYR have Captain America or Wolverine as a personal bodyguard?

251 WYR swing on a star or carry moonbeams home in a jar?

252 WYR go on a cruise with friends or stay at a luxury private island resort with family members?

253   WYR only listen to music from the 1980s or only watch movies from the 1980s?

254   WYR shoot lightning from your fingers or turn things to ice with your stare?

255   WYR be able to wash your face like a cat or scratch behind your ears like a dog?

256   WYR slither like a snake or hop like a frog?

257   WYR noisy neighbors kept you awake or nosy neighbors watched your every move?

258   WYR have shorter work hours each week or longer vacations each year?

259   WYR communicate by smoke signals or by carrier pigeon?

260   WYR work in a team or work alone?

261   WYR live in a beach house or a mountain chalet?

262   WYR hear the bad news or the good news first?

263   WYR dress head to toe in tartan or in a paisley pattern?

264   WYR be your own boss or work for an awesome boss?

265   WYR have a pain in your neck or have a pain in your butt?

266   WYR be a wealthy person living in 1760 or be on an average income living in 1960?

267   WYR be trapped in an elevator with someone who picks and flicks or someone who farts incessantly?

268   WYR be a celebrity chef or have a personal chef?

269   WYR be in the crowd at a big sports game or at home watching the game live on TV?

270   WYR be the worm that turned or the fish that got away?

271   WYR invent an instant weight-loss plan that works or an anti-aging cream that works?

272   WYR stand out from the crowd or blend into the background?

273 WYR wear your underpants on the outside like Superman or wear a mask like the Lone Ranger?

274 WYR cut your hand off to escape death or abandon a friend in danger to escape death?

275 WYR have no say in what you eat or no say in what you watch on TV?

276 WYR be the nerd who cracks the code to save the world or the action hero who kills off the baddies?

277 WYR your flight was canceled or you lost your luggage?

278 WYR have a koala cling to your leg or a sloth hang around your neck?

279 WYR live next door to a rooster that crows at dawn or a dog that howls at midnight?

280 WYR never know who your father is or discover your father is serving a life sentence in prison?

281 WYR sprout feathers like a cockatoo on your head or have bumblebee-striped hair?

282 WYR have a toothache or an earache for a week?

283 WYR color within the lines or think outside the box?

284 WYR wear a sleeping cat or a sleeping squirrel as a hat?

285 WYR be the man in the moon or the cow that jumped over the moon?

286 WYR be the shortest person on the basketball team or the tallest person in the "how many people in a Minivan" team?

287 WYR be the star player in the losing team or on the subs bench in the winning team?

288 WYR have too little time and so much to do or have too little to do and so much time?

289 WYR be a good player in a televised sport or a champion player in a lesser-known sport?

290 WYR be attracted to light like a moth or get sunburned when you sit under an electric light?

291 WYR have a private pilot's license or be able to charter a private jet whenever you want?

292 WYR time travel to meet a world leader of the past or a world leader fifty years into the future?

293 WYR join a traveling circus or join the French Foreign Legion?

294 WYR be the bee's knees or the cat's pajamas?

295 WYR have an indoor job or an outdoor job?

296 WYR try to leave a restaurant without paying or get pranked with a bucket of water when you go through a door?

297 WYR have a cocktail named after you or a cologne named after you?

298 WYR be the first person to step onto the rickety rope bridge or the last person in line for the lifeboat?

299 WYR be famous and constantly hounded by paparazzi or famous and almost forgotten by the press?

300 WYR shave your head or never brush your hair again?

301 WYR upcycle old furniture or be minimalist with very little furniture?

302 WYR be stranded in an airport for forty-eight hours or stuck at home for four days without power?

303 WYR be in an arranged marriage or remain single for life?

304 WYR be pulled from the crowd to sing at a country music festival or to be a participant in a hypnotist's act?

305 WYR babysit a crying baby or have a noisy teenage houseguest?

306 WYR be the frosting on the cake or the jelly in the donut?

307 WYR get dog poop on your shoe or sand in your eye?

308 WYR be a Greyhound bus driver or a subway train driver?

309 WYR meet the cast of *Friends* at Central Perk or the cast of *Cheers* at Cheers?

310 WYR be a flea on a dog or a crocodile bird in a crocodile's mouth?

311 WYR go speed dating or have a friend set you up on a blind date?

312 WYR wear the same underpants or the same socks for two days?

313 WYR be a ventriloquist's dummy or a puppet on a string?

314 WYR slide down the banister or swing from the chandelier?

315 WYR have a fairy godmother or have Santa Claus as your uncle?

316 WYR ride on the Polar Express or the Hogwarts Express?

317 WYR learn how to eat fire or learn how to ride a motorcycle wall of death?

318 WYR ride a unicorn or swim with a mermaid?

319 WYR be the pet sitter for 101 Dalmatians or the babysitter for the old woman who lived in a shoe?

320 WYR tiptoe through the tulips or walk on the wild side?

321 WYR be able to see through walls or listen in on conversations a block away?

322 WYR get yelled at by a stranger every day or buy a coffee for a stranger every day?

323 WYR get brain freeze every time you eat or bite your tongue every time you eat?

324 WYR swim with dolphins or soar with eagles?

325 WYR have an Elf on the Shelf or toilet roll on the shelf?

326 WYR try to walk up a slippery slope or climb a greasy pole?

327 WYR know the answer to every riddle or know how to order beer and pizza in every language?

328 WYR have a hairless cat or a hairless dog?

329 WYR be a salty dog or the cat that got the cream?

330 WYR have a real lightsaber or a real Excalibur?

331 WYR dress only in leisure wear or only in formal wear for the rest of your life?

332 WYR spend three weeks in prison or six weeks under house arrest?

333 WYR have a healing finger like E.T. or self-healing powers like Wolverine?

334 WYR get rid of Times New Roman font or Arial font?

335 WYR be able to redesign your body every day like the Sims or get designer clothes for free?

336 WYR have the highest number of followers on Twitter or on TikTok?

337 WYR your seat at a restaurant table was a little too low or a little too high?

338 WYR wash the cut on your hand in lemon juice and salt or get lemon juice in your eye?

339 WYR get punched by Mike Tyson or kicked by Bruce Lee?

340 WYR suffer from one long-term health condition or go through life believing you have every condition?

341 WYR have Cheetos dust on your fingers forever or the smell of onions on your fingers forever?

342 WYR never hit your funny bone again or never stub your toe again?

343 WYR have Batman's Batmobile or Iron Man's suit?

344 WYR hear Simon Cowell critique Gordon Ramsay's singing or Gordon Ramsay critique Simon Cowell's cooking?

345 WYR be the manager of a store with underperforming employees or be one of the underperforming employees?

346 WYR breathe fire like a dragon or rise from the flames like a phoenix?

347 WYR go to Hogwarts School of Witchcraft and Wizardry or Xavier's School for Gifted Youngsters?

348 WYR be tickled for five minutes every day or be made to listen to one-liner jokes for ten minutes every day?

349 WYR be indestructible or invisible?

350 WYR spend an afternoon with Captain Hook or Darth Vader?

351 WYR have no thumbs or no fingers?

352 WYR slip on a banana peel and fall on your butt or step barefoot on a Lego brick?

353 WYR be a toy soldier or a toy car for a day?

354 WYR be Rick-rolled or be a famous internet troll?

355 WYR have hair like Rapunzel or wings like Tinkerbell?

356 WYR be a Jedi or a Minion?

357 WYR be a bull in a china shop or as timid as a mouse?

358 WYR have your face on the front cover of a magazine or your name on the front of a book?

359 WYR sharks could walk on land or lions could swim underwater?

360 WYR prove the existence of the Loch Ness Monster or leprechauns?

361 WYR be hugely famous for a few years in your lifetime or achieve fame after your death?

362 WYR have a real Millennium Falcon or a real time-traveling DeLorean?

363 WYR be able to control light switches or switch TV channels using your mind?

364 WYR only be able to speak to give orders or only be able to walk by marching?

365 WYR have a snot-and-earwax smoothie or a fish-gut-and-toe-cheese sandwich?

366 WYR be a volcano or a waterfall?

367 WYR be green with envy or red with anger?

368 WYR smell the aroma of freshly baked bread or freshly cut flowers?

369 WYR be able to talk to trees or interpret whale song?

370 WYR have no eyebrows or super-long nasal hair?

371 WYR eat a whole raw onion or drink a raw-egg shake?

372 WYR be a lion in captivity or a bear in the wild in hunting season?

373 WYR only be able to eat raw foods or only be able to eat canned foods?

374 WYR have an actual button for a nose or a clown's nose?

375 WYR be able to see in the dark like a cat or use echolocation like a bat?

376 WYR have a sniffly cold three times a year or a heavy cold once a year?

377 WYR be able to move things with your mind or read other people's minds?

378 WYR search for a needle in a haystack or go on a wild goose chase?

379 WYR be flavor of the month or an acquired taste?

380 WYR have wings like a griffin or a tail like a dragon?

381 WYR your milkshake was too warm or your coffee too cold?

382 WYR have no sense of humor or have no one ever laugh at your jokes?

383 WYR be a street artist or street musician?

384 WYR have multiple piercings on your face or a tattoo on your face?

385 WYR hear a bump in the night or hear a scratching sound in the night?

386 WYR have dandruff or have a bad hair day every other day?

387 WYR live in an old-fashioned windmill or an ancient castle with a moat?

388 WYR only be able to move around on a skateboard or on roller skates?

389 WYR never wear socks or always wear odd socks?

390 WYR have tennis elbow or housemaid's knee?

391 WYR never cry again or never dance again?

392 WYR have a film crew follow your every move for a week or have zero contact with anyone for a week?

393 WYR fly first class for free for a year or fly economy class for free for ten years?

394 WYR be able to pitch a baseball at 100 mph or ace a tennis serve at 150 mph?

395 WYR never be able to run again or never be able to sing again?

396 WYR spend one hour in a public library every day or two hours in a public swimming pool once a week?

397 WYR die surrounded by family at the age of forty or outlive most of your family and die at the age of 104?

398 WYR have no eyelashes or no fingernails?

399 WYR be able to spin your head like an owl or change color like a chameleon?

400 WYR wake up on a raft in the middle of the ocean or on a blanket in the middle of a desert?

401 WYR have four arms and no legs or four legs and no arms?

402 WYR eat a snail a day or a giant centipede once a month?

403 WYR live in your dream house in your least favorite location or an ugly house in your favorite location?

404 WYR be covered in scales for two full days or be covered in fur from 6 pm to 6 am for a week?

405 WYR see no daylight for a month or be under nighttime curfew for a month?

406 WYR walk barefoot in a city or walk barefoot in a jungle?

407 WYR be below-average height or earn a below-average income?

408 WYR be a world-champion yodeler or a world-champion thumb wrestler?

409 WYR paint the outside of your house neon pink or share your house with a colony of bats?

410 WYR go from riches to rags or from A-lister to nobody?

411 WYR get great grades at school without trying or be great at all sports without trying?

412 WYR the wind was on your back when you cycled or you had clear roads when driving?

413 WYR have your hands tied behind your back or your ankles tied together?

414 WYR discover a dark family secret or have a skeleton in your closet revealed?

415 WYR it rained for forty days and forty nights or a gale-force wind blew for forty days and forty nights?

416 WYR have a personal chef or a personal maid?

417 WYR be a circus performer or a catwalk model?

418 WYR buy no new clothes for a year or have new clothes every day chosen for you by someone else?

419 WYR be the butt of a joke or be the last person to get the joke?

420 WYR be an Olympic archer or a skilled knife thrower?

421 WYR wear shoes that pinch or underpants a size too small?

422 WYR be a record-breaker or a champion breakdancer?

423 WYR giant pandas were the size of penguins or Chihuahuas were the size of lions?

424 WYR hang out with Puss in Boots or with Pinocchio?

425 WYR your friend's worst habit was nail biting or lip smacking?

426 WYR be a competitor in underwater hockey or extreme ironing?

427 WYR be the worst singer or the worst dancer in a pop band?

428 WYR not know where your next meal is coming from or not know where you're sleeping tonight?

429 WYR binge watch every *Harry Potter* movie or every *Looney Tunes* cartoon ever made?

430 WYR know how to train your dragon or how to do the expelliarmus spell?

431 WYR have nonstop diarrhea for two days or vomit every morning for two weeks?

432 WYR sleep fully clothed (including shoes) or sleep with a bright spotlight on you?

433 WYR make horse hoof noises with coconut shells as you walk or wear squeaking clown shoes?

434 WYR struggle to wake up every morning or struggle to get to sleep every night?

435 WYR be joined by the neighborhood stray dogs when you go for a jog or by a group of jogging moms with strollers?

436 WYR only get to change your clothes once a week or have a shower once a week?

437 WYR everything left a bad taste in your mouth or everything had a bad smell?

438 WYR never get another paper cut or never burn your tongue again?

439 WYR be hungry or be tired?

440 WYR be guaranteed never to fart in public or never say the wrong thing again?

441 WYR have an awesome-looking car that can only reach 60 mph or a rust bucket that can reach 200 mph?

442 WYR have an amazing body and a plain face or a gorgeous face and a not-so-great body?

443 WYR be trapped in a room full of party balloons and sharp-clawed kittens or a room full of toddlers with kazoos?

444 WYR have a credit card with a $10,000 limit or $1,000 cash?

445 WYR someone rained on your parade or be told you are a wet blanket?

446 WYR get drive-thru meals for free or free amusement park entry for life?

447 WYR never get another spam email or another spam phone call?

448 WYR live in the middle of nowhere or live and work in the center of a busy metropolis?

449 WYR rent a residence in three different cities or own one house in your hometown?

450 WYR ride a rollercoaster or ride the waves?

451 WYR look twenty-one years old physically or feel twenty-one years old mentally?

452 WYR be able to bounce on clouds or slide down a rainbow?

453 WYR be a black belt in karate or a tai chi master?

454 WYR be a one-hit wonder as a best-selling author or as the singer of a chart-topping novelty song?

455 WYR be a contestant on a TV game show or a reality TV survival show?

456 WYR be an inner-city cop or an inner-city high school teacher?

457 WYR meet Wyatt Earp or Abraham Lincoln?

458 WYR be able to snap your fingers and change your eye color or your hair color?

459 WYR be in the history books as a renowned scientist or a renowned artist?

460 WYR be a first-time parent at the age of eighteen or the age of forty?

461 WYR have blacksmithing skills or surgical skills?

462 WYR have too many friends or too few?

463   WYR sing in front of friends or in front of strangers?

464   WYR be friends with Willy Wonka or Sherlock Holmes?

465   WYR be the cat with the fiddle or the dish that ran away with the spoon?

466   WYR have retractable claws or razor-sharp teeth?

467   WYR accidentally shoot yourself in the foot or chop off a finger?

468   WYR always eat waffles for breakfast or always eat pizza for lunch?

469   WYR be very talented or extremely lucky?

470   WYR be the funniest person in your class at school or the smartest person in your workplace?

471   WYR live with messy but fun housemates or tidy but boring housemates?

472   WYR have a mouth like a cat's butt or have your eyes switch places with your nipples?

473   WYR see a ghostly apparition or feel a presence in your bedroom at night?

474   WYR never be able to fully close your mouth or never fully open one eye?

475   WYR go surfing or surf the internet?

476   WYR have unlimited credit or endless battery charge on your phone?

477   WYR live without electricity for two days or live without hot food for a week?

478   WYR have cosmetic surgery to change your nose or change your teeth?

479   WYR walk barefoot across a floor of broken glass or step barefoot on one upturned thumb tack?

480   WYR never swim in the sea again or never sled in the snow again?

481   WYR never be in another awkward silence or never fill out an application form ever again?

482 WYR have no air conditioning or no music in your car?

483 WYR share a toothbrush with a friend or borrow used underwear from a friend?

484 WYR literally have eyes in the back of your head or literally have lightning reflexes?

485 WYR be twice your weight or half your height?

486 WYR be given $10,000 today or $1 million in ten years' time?

487 WYR never get married or never have a best friend?

488 WYR be a farmer or a podiatrist?

489 WYR rescue the three-legged puppy or the one-eyed kitten from the animal shelter?

490 WYR have been a pioneer on a wagon train or a team member of the Apollo 11 moon mission?

491 WYR be the brightest star in the sky or the tallest mountain in the range?

492 WYR find your forgotten stash of candy or a forgotten box of old photographs?

493 WYR see the northern lights or a total eclipse of the sun?

494 WYR be able to change the ending of the last movie you saw or change the actors in the lead roles?

495 WYR find proof of alien life or find proof there's no other life in the universe?

496 WYR be quarantined for three months alone or with extended family members?

497 WYR have no toaster or no blender in your kitchen?

498 WYR be itchy or be cold?

499 WYR have an operatic singing voice or a raspy, rock singer voice?

500 WYR sleep sitting up or sleep lying down but unable to change position?

501 WYR have only spring and fall or only summer and winter?

502 WYR sing like a bird instead of talking or talk like Chewbacca?

503 WYR be a taxi driver in New York or an ice road trucker in Alaska?

504 WYR wake up to find your hair had fallen out or your teeth had fallen out?

505 WYR make the world's best bagels or the world's best pretzels?

506 WYR be the sharpest tool in the box or the cutest puppy in the litter?

507 WYR wear a swimsuit and sunscreen in Antarctica or a swimsuit and no sunscreen in the Sahara?

508 WYR sit in a room with 10,000 spiders or eat 100 spiders?

509 WYR be typecast as a rom-com sweetie or an evil villain?

510 WYR be the princess in "The Princess and the Pea" or one of the Twelve Dancing Princesses?

511 WYR be an @ symbol or an exclamation point?

512 WYR have super-strength by night or a photographic memory by day?

513 WYR have eggy burps or garlic breath?

514 WYR be a Formula One driver or a Red Bull Air Race pilot?

515 WYR chop onions or have sticky fingers?

516 WYR have a feather tickle your nose or tickle your feet?

517 WYR be a sword swallower or a human cannonball?

518 WYR have a frantic Friday or a manic Monday?

519 WYR use 1960s slang or wear 1990s fashion?

520 WYR hand-stitch 1,000 sequins onto a gown or handwash your clothes for a week?

521 WYR be a dog that jumps through hoops of fire or a squirrel that crosses a tightrope?

522 WYR hang out at the Batcave under Wayne Manor or the Thunderbird secret base on Tracy Island?

523 WYR have reflective eyes or glow-in-the-dark hands?

524 WYR be in prison for a year or homeless for a year?

525 WYR have sweaty palms or sweaty armpits on a first date?

526 WYR never dance again or dance nonstop for forty-eight hours?

527 WYR have tunnel vision in color or clear vision in black and white only?

528 WYR be able to ride a unicycle or spin plates?

529 WYR never be in debt or never eat ice cream again?

530 WYR have an excellent poker face or wear your heart on your sleeve?

531 WYR find a dragon's treasure or a pirate's treasure?

532 WYR live in a world with giant earthworms or giant birds?

533 WYR have a car that never wears out or never have to pay for fuel at a filling station?

534 WYR be chased by a clown or a billy goat?

535 WYR have no taste buds or be color blind?

536 WYR be limited to 140 characters of text per day instead of talking or only be able to communicate using emojis?

537 WYR never see your face in a mirror again or never remember anyone's name other than your own?

538 WYR have free access to every circus for life or free access to every gym for a year?

539 WYR be an organ donor or donate your body to science?

540 WYR be stuck in an elevator with two grumpy people or one sweet person with two smelly dogs?

541 WYR snort like a pig when you laugh or bray like a donkey when you laugh?

542 WYR only age from the neck up or the neck down?

543 WYR be the Sandman or the Tooth Fairy?

544 WYR have the power to remove yourself from embarrassing situations or the power to move objects with your mind?

545 WYR hold an octopus or a jellyfish?

546 WYR be able to bring the pictures you draw to life or be able to step into the pictures in storybooks?

547 WYR be deaf in one ear or blind in one eye?

548 WYR be a banana smoothie or a banana muffin?

549 WYR be granted three wishes that can't include money or given $1 million a year for three years?

550 WYR have everyone laugh at you for farting or be the only one to laugh when someone else farts?

551 WYR wear a mohawk hairstyle for a month or clown makeup every day for a month?

552 WYR control gravity or control time?

553 WYR be hopelessly underdressed or more than fashionably late for important events?

554 WYR be all-powerful or all-knowing?

555 WYR go back in time and have VIP tickets to see Prince in concert or Freddie Mercury in concert?

556 WYR have a huge home with no yard or a tiny home with a huge yard?

557 WYR be able to shapeshift into other living things or into inanimate objects?

558 WYR be a James Bond villain or a Disney villain?

559 WYR be able to switch your sense of smell on and off or switch your emotions on and off?

560 WYR have an ugly phone with awesome features or an awesome-looking phone with only standard features?

561 WYR choose cheesecake or fudge if only one could exist?

562 WYR have your last phone conversation broadcast on national radio or your last thought appear in words over your head?

563 WYR retake your driving test every year or retake high school tests every five years?

564 WYR end animal testing or ban zoos?

565 WYR play Dungeons and Dragons or Monopoly for a full day?

566 WYR invent a solution to world pollution or world hunger?

567 WYR save the last tree on Earth from destruction or save the Siberian tiger from extinction?

568 WYR be able to charge your phone from your belly button or have a third eye in your fingertip?

569 WYR both your feet were left feet or your hands were left hands?

570 WYR be attacked by a giant snake or an angry piranha?

571 WYR be a firefighter or a rescue helicopter pilot?

572 WYR be part of a bobsled team or an acrobatic display team?

573 WYR be able to join the Mad Hatter's tea party or a teddy bears' picnic?

574 WYR hang out with the Pink Panther or the Black Panther?

575 WYR sing the songs from *The Lion King* or *The Jungle Book*?

576 WYR only be able to go to Justin Bieber concerts or Slipknot concerts?

577 WYR go to work in your party clothes or go to a party in your work clothes?

578 WYR be one of the Fab Four (The Beatles) or one of the Fantastic Four (Marvel)?

579 WYR be able to move at *The Matrix*'s "bullet time" speed or *X-Men*'s Quicksilver speed at will?

580 WYR save a stranger's life by giving CPR or help a stranger give birth?

581 WYR sit in a bathtub of Nutella or maple syrup?

582 WYR get dressed in the dark or wear your clothes back to front?

583 WYR avoid black cats crossing your path or walking under ladders?

584 WYR work for a furniture removal company or a graffiti removal company?

585 WYR be Little Bo Peep or Miss Muffet?

586 WYR be able to magically lower the volume of crying babies in public places or traffic noise on the street?

587 WYR live in a mole hole or a bird's nest?

588 WYR go swimming with your socks on or wear socks with sandals?

589 WYR have a sing-off with Mariah Carey or a dance-off with Michael Jackson?

590 WYR see a rat in your kitchen or a bat in your bedroom?

591 WYR poke yourself in the eye or bite your tongue?

592 WYR never get stuck in traffic again or never struggle to find a parking spot again?

593 WYR sleep in a doghouse or have a slobbery dog sleep in your bed?

594 WYR breathe like Darth Vader or talk like Mickey Mouse?

595 WYR be the Bionic Man or Bionic Bunny?

596 WYR work in Silicon Valley or Hollywood?

597 WYR be a beekeeper or bookkeeper?

598 WYR spend a day in the life of *Downton Abbey* characters or *Outlander* characters?

599 WYR have Raymond Babbitt's (*Rain Man*) savant abilities or David Copperfield's illusionist abilities?

600 WYR change the ending to the story of *Beauty and the Beast* or "Little Red Riding Hood"?

601 WYR be a horse and dog trainer or a Pokémon trainer?

602 WYR have the powers of Tinkerbell in *Peter Pan* or Elsa in *Frozen*?

603 WYR lose control of your legs every time you sneeze or every time you hear someone else sneeze?

604 WYR wear wet jeans until they dry out or go ice skating with wet hair?

605 WYR burn food or burn your fingers every time you cook?

606 WYR build a Meccano (Erector) scale model of the Eiffel Tower or the Golden Gate Bridge?

607 WYR have a scorpion's tail or a rattlesnake's tail?

608 WYR be an orchestral conductor or the timpani (kettledrums) player in an orchestra?

609 WYR jump rope or bounce on a trampoline?

610 WYR feed the birds or water the plants?

611 WYR walk through a giant cobweb or wade barefoot through frog spawn?

612 WYR be pranked with worms as spaghetti or maggots as rice?

613 WYR spend a rainy afternoon in a library or in a museum?

614 WYR be able to visit Jurassic Park for real or be in *Night at the Museum* for real?

615 WYR have *Mission: Impossible* theme play every time you pee or the *Hawaii Five-O* theme?

616 WYR spend a full day wearing snowshoes or wearing a beekeeper's hat?

617 WYR sing-along so hard your voice cracks or laugh so hard your sides hurt?

618 WYR avoid stepping on cracks on sidewalks or avoid opening an umbrella indoors?

619   WYR be a pangolin or a penguin?

620   WYR be a street sweeper or a crewmember on a navy minesweeper?

621   WYR be a passenger stepping off the Mayflower into the New World or be Christopher Columbus setting sail across the Atlantic?

622   WYR have fifteen children or fifteen dogs?

623   WYR have an easy job working for someone else or work for yourself but work really hard?

624   WYR be a chicken that barks like a dog or a hamster that clicks like a dolphin?

625   WYR sketch and doodle or color?

626   WYR be able to solve any math equation or able to fix any household gadget?

627   WYR go out without brushing your hair or without brushing your teeth?

628   WYR fight a Roman gladiator or a samurai warrior?

629   WYR have a cassette-playing Sony Walkman instead of music downloads or a landline instead of a smartphone?

630   WYR comfort-eat with a whole carton of ice cream or a whole bucket of chicken wings?

631   WYR be a pirate or a ninja for the weekend?

632   WYR drink water from the cat's water bowl or pee in the litter box?

633   WYR have an annoying song stuck in your head or the feeling you're about to sneeze for an hour?

634   WYR do only indoor activities every weekend or only outdoor activities every weekend?

635   WYR have a personal trainer or a personal chauffeur?

636   WYR only eat sushi or only eat TV dinners?

637   WYR have the strength of Superman or the speed of The Flash?

638   WYR sleep on a public bathroom floor or on poison ivy?

639   WYR learn an alien language or teach your language to an alien?

640   WYR buy more than you need at the grocery store or forget the one thing you need?

641   WYR lose your short-term memory or your long-term memory?

642   WYR have rain on your wedding day or only have spoons when you need a knife?

643   WYR be able to predict your own future or the future of the world?

644   WYR live with a ghost in your house or be a ghost in someone else's house?

645   WYR have a bath in dirty dishwater or wash dishes in dirty bathwater?

646   WYR be able to wipe your own memory or wipe someone else's memory, *Men in Black*-style?

647   WYR wear just one color or a mix of at least three colors every day?

648   WYR be ignored or have everything you say and do criticized?

649   WYR "Go West" with the Pet Shop Boys or stay at the "Hotel California" with the Eagles?

650   WYR clean up after every party you attend or never go to another party?

651   WYR only eat desserts for a year or not eat any desserts for two years?

652   WYR wear only neon pink or only neon yellow for a year?

653   WYR have a tennis lesson with Serena Williams or a golf lesson with Tiger Woods?

654   WYR be a punk rocker or a pink pony?

655   WYR live in a glass house with no blinds or a house with no windows?

656 WYR spectate at a *Punch and Judy* puppet show or dance at a barn dance?

657 WYR score the winning goal in the World Cup or be the coach of the winning team in the World Cup?

658 WYR have no power or no water in your home for a week?

659 WYR wake up in the gorilla enclosure in a zoo or in the wolf zone of a safari park?

660 WYR be able to make vanish inconsiderate drivers or people who talk loudly on their phones in public places?

661 WYR never listen to music or only be able to listen to the same three songs?

662 WYR have a string of chart-topping hits or have a long musical career with no No. 1 hits?

663 WYR snack on chicken nuggets or donut holes?

664 WYR go back in time to meet Mohammad Ali in his prime or Jesse Owens in his prime?

665 WYR be a horse whisperer or a lion tamer?

666 WYR be a social media influencer or a community hero?

667 WYR look young when you're desperate to be older or look your age when you want to be younger?

668 WYR give or take bad advice?

669 WYR live forever but look your age or always look young but live an average length of life?

670 WYR have a fear of heights that keeps you on the first floor or a fear of the dark that means lights must stay on?

671 WYR become a cat or a dog?

672 WYR have an escalator or a travelator (moving walkway) in your home?

673 WYR live in a *Jetsons*-style home or a *Flintstones*-style home?

674 WYR have the grace of a swan or the memory of an elephant?

675 WYR ride on the top deck of a double-decker bus or on the back of an elephant?

676 WYR have a guided tour of The White House or Buckingham Palace?

677 WYR have your decisions made for you by other people or by tossing a coin?

678 WYR drink a gallon of ketchup or chew gum you found stuck under a table?

679 WYR lose all the photos on your smartphone or lose your tickets for the big game?

680 WYR have ears that can record what you hear or eyes that can record what you see?

681 WYR have unlimited storage space in your home or on your computer?

682 WYR be a flightless bird or a non-venomous snake?

683 WYR only be able to get into your car through a window or into your home through a window?

684 WYR have ants in your pants or bugs in your bed?

685 WYR have a frozen shoulder or be given the cold shoulder?

686 WYR be able to pause time once a day or go back ten seconds once a day at will?

687 WYR be a super sleuth or a super safecracker?

688 WYR eat what you want and never be overweight or never exercise and always be fit?

689 WYR have a personal robot or a flying carpet?

690 WYR be a practicing doctor or a medical researcher?

691 WYR fly a kite or fly in the face of danger?

692 WYR be stung by a bee or by ten mosquitos?

693 WYR have more time or more money?

694 WYR be able to change the length of your hair at will or snap your fingers to change outfits?

695 WYR meet a superhero or a cartoon character?

696 WYR be a spelling bee champion or a baton twirling champion?

697 WYR be an underwater creature with wings or a land animal with gills?

698 WYR spend a day playing paintball or laser tag?

699 WYR have a bugle fanfare as you enter a room or a drum roll before you speak?

700 WYR have breakfast at Tiffany's or tea at The Ritz?

701 WYR wallow in mud pie or chocolate pudding?

702 WYR kiss a dirty trashcan or a frog?

703 WYR shovel snow for thirty minutes twice a day or rake leaves for one hour once a day?

704 WYR be able to dodge anything no matter how fast it's moving or be able ask any three questions and have them answered accurately?

705 WYR brush your teeth with soap or curdled milk?

706 WYR know the lyrics to every song or know the moves to every dance?

707 WYR have one puppy or five kittens?

708 WYR be a maid for the untidiest person in the world or a chef for the fussiest eater in the world?

709 WYR have a magic button that could stop other people from talking or stop other people from moving?

710 WYR never feel pain or have your loved ones never feel pain?

711 WYR have crooked white teeth or straight yellow-stained teeth?

712 WYR fart loudly fifty times every day or pee your pants in public once a year?

713 WYR be the captain of a debate team or the captain of a sports team?

714 WYR have five cavities or five warts?

715 WYR see something no one else can see or not see something everyone else can see?

716 WYR wear a superhero cape or a pirate eyepatch?

717 WYR travel at the speed of light or relax at the speed of a sloth?

718 WYR drink out of a five-gallon bucket or a thimble?

719 WYR be able to see smells or smell sounds?

720 WYR be told you're adopted or that your siblings are adopted?

721 WYR have a house made of gingerbread or a tree that grows candy canes?

722 WYR be able to sketch things into existence or erase existing things with an eraser?

723 WYR run everywhere in a potato sack or always sleep in a sleeping bag?

724 WYR your breath smelled of garlic or you had food stains on your clothes?

725 WYR have the power to push things away using your eyes or pull things towards you using your eyes?

726 WYR accidentally spoil a movie for someone or have someone spoil a movie for you?

727 WYR be able to purr like a cat or trumpet like an elephant?

728 WYR have Pinocchio's nose or Dumbo's ears?

729 WYR be showered with Silly String or with confetti?

730 WYR walk on your hands or eat with your feet?

731 WYR own a prickly pet or a slimy pet?

732 WYR have antennae like a bug or smell with your tongue like a snake?

733 WYR be obliged to announce the imminent arrival of every burp or every fart before you do it?

734 WYR be trapped in a small space with five capuchin monkeys or twenty people?

735 WYR live on a pig's diet for a week or a shark's diet for a week?

736 WYR have a private paradise island or a private amusement park?

737 WYR live one long life of a thousand years or live ten different lives, each lasting a hundred years?

738 WYR have two spoonfuls of sugar or one spoonful of salt sprinkled on every meal you eat?

739 WYR be under the attack of a hundred snowballs or a hundred water balloons?

740 WYR stick your hand in a bucket of freezing cold water or a bucket of warm fish guts?

741 WYR please others or please yourself?

742 WYR drink through your ears or eat through your belly button?

743 WYR have the power to shrink everything at will or make things double in size?

744 WYR trip and fall running toward someone or running away from someone?

745 WYR have soda spray out your mouth or come down your nose when you laugh?

746 WYR be the first person to explore a planet or be the inventor of a drug that cures a deadly disease?

747 WYR be the last to know good news or the first to know bad news?

748 WYR look like a magazine front-cover model or be totally comfortable in your own skin?

749 WYR be the target for dodgeball practice or get six raw eggs cracked open on your head?

750 WYR run through sprinklers for fun or swing on a tree rope?

751 WYR use your non-dominant hand to write or to eat?

752 WYR never get tired or never have to go to the bathroom?

753 WYR go to clown school or agricultural college?

754 WYR grow new teeth like a shark or wear down your constantly growing teeth like a beaver?

755 WYR wear shoes on the wrong feet or shoes two sizes too big?

756 WYR catch the biggest fish on a fishing trip or the highest number of small fish?

757 WYR teleport to a different dimension or to a different country in this dimension?

758 WYR be the superhero or the superhero's indispensable sidekick?

759 WYR be bulletproof or have the power to catch bullets in your hands?

760 WYR be able to fly on a broomstick or have an invisibility cloak?

761 WYR have a dog's brain in a human body or a human brain in a dog's body?

762 WYR never be sad again or never be angry again?

763 WYR be a test pilot or a food tester?

764 WYR sleep with only a blanket or only a pillow?

765 WYR work in a sewage plant or a toxic chemicals plant?

766 WYR have a nose ring or a full sleeve tattoo?

767 WYR wear only flip flops in winter or only snow boots in summer?

768 WYR live in a house with a hall of mirrors or a concealed door in the bookcase?

769 WYR have to sit down all day in your job or stand up all day in your job?

770 WYR love animals but be allergic to them or not be allergic to animals but be frightened of them?

771 WYR be a 1960s hippie or a 1920s flapper?

772 WYR never be rejected ever again or never fail ever again?

773 WYR sit next to someone who snores or someone who snaps their gum on a long-haul flight?

774 WYR have a time machine or a teleport machine?

775 WYR be the director of a Hollywood blockbuster or have twenty million subscribers to your YouTube channel?

776 WYR be totally alone for a year or never be alone for a year?

777 WYR only be able to listen to rap music or songs from Broadway musicals?

778 WYR have a starring role in a TV drama or a supporting role in a Hollywood movie?

779 WYR be a game show host or a stand-up comedian?

780 WYR win an Academy Award or an Olympic medal?

781 WYR figure things out for yourself or ask for help?

782 WYR freefall into the Grand Canyon with a parachute or run across a river on the backs of alligators?

783 WYR have a booger in your nose that moves in and out when you breathe or sneeze a booger onto someone?

784 WYR have cookies or cake if you could only have one?

785 WYR be an actor doing your own stunts or a stuntman doing stunts for actors?

786 WYR suffer from unpredictable fits of giggles or spontaneous moments of talking like a pirate?

787 WYR lick the bottom of your shoe or wear someone else's sweaty socks?

788 WYR have stitches or have a dislocated shoulder popped back in without anesthetic?

789 WYR cry tears of lemonade or sneeze cheese?

790 WYR be true to yourself or fake it till you make it?

791 WYR lie to your family or lie to your friends?

792 WYR argue until the cows come home or walk away from an argument?

793 WYR get caught in a swarm of crickets or an army of ants?

794 WYR own a restaurant chain or a hotel chain?

795 WYR have a broken foot or a broken hand?

796 WYR spill a pot of silver glitter on a black carpet or a pot of paprika on a white carpet?

797 WYR be a ski instructor or a surf instructor?

798 WYR be able to navigate using the stars or tell the time using the sun?

799 WYR go back to age five with everything you know now or know now everything your future self will learn?

800 WYR be a parkour master or a master chef?

801 WYR have a hairdryer or a vacuum cleaner that lacks power?

802 WYR a movie was made of your life since the age of twenty-one or your life before the age of twenty-one?

803 WYR have constant dull pain or a constant itch?

804 WYR never be able to ask another question or never be able to answer another question?

805 WYR live in Narnia or the Pokémon universe?

806 WYR hold the world record for holding your breath or for holding the longest singing note?

807 WYR discover where the missing socks go or find $50 down the back of the sofa?

808 WYR go to work in a tutu or in traditional German lederhosen?

809 WYR read everything out loud or speak your thoughts out loud?

810   WYR do a TED talk or sing a song on stage at a concert with your favorite singer?

811   WYR communicate using only an Etch-a-Sketch or through the medium of interpretive dance?

812   WYR spend a night in a teepee or an igloo?

813   WYR blow up a hundred party balloons without a pump or wash ten cars by hand?

814   WYR lose three friends or gain an enemy?

815   WYR have duck feet or go for a swim before every meal?

816   WYR end crime or end poverty?

817   WYR be eliminated from *Survivor* or *The X Factor*?

818   WYR wake up and be unable to see your reflection in a mirror or not recognize the person you see in the mirror?

819   WYR be a barnacle on a whale or a starfish on a rock?

820   WYR get free iTunes for life or get free tickets to see your favorite band in concert?

821   WYR have it all or know it all?

822   WYR get bad sunburn or fall into stinging nettles wearing only a swimsuit?

823   WYR sleep in a hammock or sleep on a mattress on the floor?

824   WYR have a pillow fight or a midnight feast?

825   WYR visit Universal Studios or Epcot Center?

826   WYR run with bulls in Spain or walk on the Great Wall of China?

827   WYR lose your wallet or lose all the photos on your phone?

828   WYR spend the night alone in a wax museum or a morgue?

829   WYR have a face like a cat or a monkey's tail for a week?

830   WYR never move from the house you grew up in or move into a different house every two years?

831 WYR be the bull rider at the rodeo or the clown that distracts the bull when the rider falls?

832 WYR meet an Ent (*The Lord of the Rings*) or the BFG?

833 WYR wear a swim cap or a nose plug to work for a week?

834 WYR own a dragon or be a dragon?

835 WYR get your hand stuck in a jar or a pot stuck on your head?

836 WYR hold a grudge or let bygones be bygones?

837 WYR talk like Daffy Duck or Bugs Bunny?

838 WYR live a dog's life or have a cat's nine lives?

839 WYR drink hot sauce or eat a stick of butter?

840 WYR never laugh again or sound like Woody Woodpecker every time you laughed?

841 WYR sit through a movie you're not enjoying or pay for a meal you don't enjoy?

842 WYR be a real-world magician or a wizard in a fantasy world?

843 WYR wake up as a character in your favorite anime or wake up to a pot of gold on your pillow?

844 WYR have a missing finger or an extra toe?

845 WYR go to prison for your best friend's crime or have your best friend go to prison for your crime?

846 WYR everyone had to backflip into meeting rooms or cartwheel out of meeting rooms?

847 WYR have a big bedroom or a big bed?

848 WYR blow your own horn or hide your light under a bushel?

849 WYR eat a ladybug or be a litterbug?

850 WYR be the tree or the tree house?

851 WYR have a suitcase full of dollars or a blood-stained knife in your car when pulled over by a police officer?

852 WYR misread everything you read or mispronounce everything you say?

853 WYR be able to solve every sudoku puzzle or complete every crossword?

854 WYR be Highlander (Connor MacLeod) or Wolverine?

855 WYR be a traditional Chinese lion dancer or dance with your dog?

856 WYR get eggs fresh from your own chickens or milk fresh from your own cow?

857 WYR have Uncle Buck or Mrs. Doubtfire as your babysitter?

858 WYR never be credited or take the credit for someone else's efforts?

859 WYR have lived in the times of *Gone with the Wind* or the times of *Casablanca*?

860 WYR read *War and Peace* in its entirety or run two marathons?

861 WYR do your laundry by hand for a week or cut an acre of grass with a manual push mower?

862 WYR have green fingers or blue blood?

863 WYR work eight hours a day in a job you love or four hours a day in a job you hate?

864 WYR everyone looked the same or everyone had the same name?

865 WYR have two kittens in mittens or one puss in boots?

866 WYR walk a mile in someone else's shoes or a mile in stilettos?

867 WYR roast chestnuts on an open fire or ride a chestnut horse?

868 WYR build a bridge or burn a bridge?

869 WYR punish thieves by putting them in ye olde stocks or punish irresponsible drivers by putting them on the ducking stool?

870 WYR be reincarnated as a bee or a tree?

871 WYR have a sparrow's nest in your hair or a wasps' nest in your bedroom?

872 WYR speak in rhyme or speak in riddles?

873 WYR have first pick or have the last laugh?

874 WYR speak an ancient (dead) language or construct a new language?

875 WYR be held in high regard by your parents or by your friends?

876 WYR be happy and you know it or be beautiful and not know it?

877 WYR have a wolf at the door or not be able to get your foot in the door?

878 WYR make an entrance or pussyfoot around?

879 WYR have a flying carpet or a car that can drive underwater?

880 WYR pit yourself against Canadian wildlife or Australian wildlife in a survival situation?

881 WYR have a bad taste in your mouth or smell a bit funky?

882 WYR have Old MacDonald's Farm or Winnie the Pooh's Hundred Acre Wood?

883 WYR be snug as a bug in a rug or cool as a cucumber?

884 WYR be Clark Kent without his Superman powers or Peter Parker without his Spiderman powers?

885 WYR be anonymous or eponymous and give your name to something?

886 WYR be a prisoner in Azkaban or Alcatraz?

887 WYR get your way or go with the flow?

888 WYR be an average person in the present or a king of a large country 2500 years ago?

889 WYR risk eating tomato-based pasta sauce or drinking red berry juice when wearing an all-white outfit?

890 WYR have the power to control your dreams or control the dreams of others?

891 WYR drink milk straight from a cow or eat raw steak?

892   WYR be a mad scientist or a computer-hacking genius?

893   WYR drive a tank or pilot a fighter jet?

894   WYR ride into battle on a warhorse or in a chariot?

895   WYR be able to ice skate on sidewalks or have waterslides on sidewalks?

896   WYR have a cat with nine tails or a llama with two heads?

897   WYR have a pet that can talk to you (only you) or a pet that never dies?

898   WYR celebrate Thanksgiving twice a year or the 4th of July twice a year?

899   WYR have an invisibility cloak or a spaceship with a cloaking device?

900   WYR be a space pirate or an eighteenth-century smuggler?

901   WYR be a police officer with a flying motorcycle or a police officer with a talking dog?

902   WYR be feared by all or loved by all?

903   WYR never be able to eat nachos again or never be able to eat Cheetos again?

904   WYR only be able to eat when it's dark outside or only be able to sleep when it's light outside?

905   WYR have a chicken that lays chocolate eggs or a cow that gives strawberry milk?

906   WYR have been in charge of building Stonehenge or the Egyptian pyramids?

907   WYR have gravy on cookies or custard on potato chips?

908   WYR live in a world with no crime or no lies?

909   WYR live in a cupboard under the stairs like Harry Potter or in a pineapple under the sea like SpongeBob SquarePants?

910   WYR your closet door led to Monstropolis (*Monsters, Inc.*) or Narnia?

911   WYR be forgetful or clumsy?

912   WYR play baseball with a basketball or football with a tennis ball?

913   WYR be a professional belly dancer or a professional limbo dancer?

914   WYR wake up to a *Planet of the Apes* world or an *Independence Day* world?

915   WYR run across America like Forrest Gump or run in the U.S. presidential election?

916   WYR wear weighted deep-sea diving boots all day or operate keyboards with your feet?

917   WYR live in a spacious one-level loft apartment or a three-story mansion?

918   WYR be a theme park ride designer or a wedding planner?

919   WYR be a wild hare or have great hair?

920   WYR bring back an extinct species or prevent another species from becoming extinct?

921   WYR have a guide dog or a guide toucan?

922   WYR be unable to talk once a day for an hour or be unable to talk for a year?

923   WYR eat a hundred apples or drink a hundred pints of milk?

924   WYR everything smelled like freshly mown grass or cotton candy?

925   WYR a house-elf moved into your bedroom or a friendly under-the-bed monster?

926   WYR become a Transformer or have rocket boots for a day?

927   WYR eat a bag of dog treats or drink a glass of hot dog water?

928   WYR a story you're writing became reality or a story you're reading became reality?

929   WYR every argument in the world was settled with rock paper scissors or the weather was decided with a coin toss?

930   WYR have a magic self-refilling fridge or be able to memorize everything you see and hear?

931   WYR exercise by walking on a treadmill or juggling oranges for thirty minutes every day?

932   WYR have Knight Rider's Kitt or Herbie the Love Bug?

933   WYR be a paramedic or a private eye?

934   WYR count out loud to a billion once or climb up the 1,576 stairs of the Empire State Building twice in one day?

935   WYR have a foam party or a BBQ on the beach?

936   WYR have fangs or a crooked smile?

937   WYR clean a public restroom without gloves or walk through a cow field without socks and shoes?

938   WYR be a full-time clown or a full-time steeplejack?

939   WYR be face to face with a shark in a submerged shark cage or eat pufferfish (fugu)?

940   WYR be a Muppet in *The Muppet Movie* or a Fraggle on *Fraggle Rock*?

941   WYR run a post office or an office supply store?

942   WYR be able to see five minutes into the future or five years into the future?

943   WYR have unshakeable will power or have a credit card with no limit?

944   WYR become a ghost or a zombie when you die?

945   WYR be the spy in a spy novel or the mole in an organization?

946   WYR be obsessive and meticulous or haphazard and nonchalant?

947   WYR have Mickey Mouse's *Fantasia* broomstick or Cinderella's helpful bluebirds?

948   WYR wear the Cat in the Hat's hat or Jack Sparrow's hat?

949   WYR be feared or be fearless?

950 WYR sweep things under the rug or risk opening a can of worms?

951 WYR never have to barf again or never have constipation ever again?

952 WYR spend the day in a beautiful location on a rainy day or a dull location on a sunny day?

953 WYR be a hamster on a wheel or a ferret in a tunnel?

954 WYR crack open a rotten egg or spill rotten milk?

955 WYR be a practical person or a dreamer?

956 WYR wake up as a giant cockroach or a giant snail?

957 WYR win a three-minute shopping cart dash in a candy store or win a lifetime pass for your local gym?

958 WYR spend a day washing glass windows or wearing glass shoes?

959 WYR have a dog named Cat or a cat that needs to be walked on a lead like a dog?

960 WYR have the eyes of a painting follow you around a room or be secretly filmed by a hidden camera?

961 WYR have a hat that turned into a helicopter or shoes that turned into a jet ski?

962 WYR ride a desert train or a ghost train?

963 WYR drink only cranberry juice or only milk?

964 WYR meet Will Smith as the Fresh Prince of Bel-Air or Agent J (*Men in Black*)?

965 WYR sticks and stones could never break your bones or names could never hurt you?

966 WYR your hair grew to ankle-length every two days or changed color every day?

967 WYR never have to sleep again or be able to take a nap whenever you want?

968 WYR love or be loved?

969 WYR have the best headphones in the world or be able to play music at any volume anywhere and anytime?

970 WYR hug or fist bump?

971 WYR all food looked the same or tasted the same?

972 WYR have to wear hi-vis clothing or a hairnet at your job?

973 WYR be liked or be respected?

974 WYR be the world's best bread maker or the world's best cake baker?

975 WYR never get another mosquito bite or never get another paper cut?

976 WYR be compelled to shout "Boogers!" or "Cowabunga!" every time you enter a building?

977 WYR have a nose the size of your fist or hands the size of your nose?

978 WYR spread mayo or strawberry jam on everything you eat?

979 WYR host a late-night TV talk show or a radio breakfast show?

980 WYR paint the town red or be tickled pink?

981 WYR be a free spirit or know your sole purpose in life?

982 WYR swim with Willy the orca or hang out with Beethoven the dog?

983 WYR be able to control when and how you laugh or when and how you cry?

984 WYR be poor but help people or become rich by hurting people?

985 WYR do whatever it takes or have the moral high ground?

986 WYR hug a tall cactus (saguaro) or roll in a nettle patch?

987 WYR visit the Little House on the Prairie or the Little Shop of Horrors?

988 WYR play Snap with cards or play games on Snapchat?

989 WYR sit in the back seat on a bus or the front seat on a rollercoaster?

990 WYR be tongue-tied or be a blabbermouth?

991 WYR have greater intelligence or greater wisdom?

992 WYR experience being your ninety-year-old self or return to being your nine-year-old self for a day?

993 WYR surprise someone by baking them a cake or have someone surprise you by jumping out of a cake?

994 WYR be the queen bee or king of the hill?

995 WYR have a song written about you or have your life story written?

996 WYR eat twenty pounds of cheese in one sitting or drink a gallon of ketchup in a day?

997 WYR be a dentist or have to visit the dentist once a month?

998 WYR kiss a jellyfish or shake hands with your worst enemy?

999 WYR be able to change the world or just change the way your life panned out in the last year?

1000 WYR have bulging eyes or bow legs?

1001 WYR know the true meaning of love or the meaning of life?

1002 WYR live in a world controlled by robots or a world with no formal education?

1003 WYR do things right or do the right thing?

1004 WYR live in a world without guns or a world without social media?

1005 WYR there was only one global language or everyone had to be multilingual?

1006 WYR be physically stronger or have better concentration abilities?

1007 WYR have total control or leave things to chance?

1008 WYR have more time or more power?

1009 WYR live under a sky with no stars at night or live under a sky with no clouds during the day?

1010 WYR campaign for free trade or fair trade?

1011 WYR have high self-esteem or always have a shoulder to cry on?

1012 WYR be a dog with its head out of a moving car window or a kitten chasing a ball of wool?

1013 WYR never be embarrassed again or never cry again?

1014 WYR already have everything you want or be able to afford anything you want?

1015 WYR never cheat or cheat only if you knew you couldn't be found out?

1016 WYR fall madly in love with everyone you meet or feel deeply suspicious of everyone you meet?

1017 WYR have great mental health but poor physical health or great physical health but poor mental health?

1018 WYR be responsible for sending an innocent person to prison or for letting a guilty person go free?

1019 WYR wake up speaking with a Russian accent or a French accent?

1020 WYR not be able to get a haircut for six months or not be able to watch TV for six months?

1021 WYR be a happy person for only fifty percent of your life or be a totally happy dog?

1022 WYR legalize euthanasia or make organ donation mandatory?

1023 WYR never have to clean a bathroom again or never have to do dishes again?

1024 WYR be the mouse that ran up the clock or the itsy-bitsy spider?

1025 WYR trust your intuition or trust the opinions of friends and family?

1026 WYR be confident as a leader or happy as a follower?

1027 WYR be able to save money or be able to give money away?

1028 WYR learn through reading or experimenting?

1029 WYR have superficial knowledge of most things or a deep knowledge of a few things?

1030 WYR eat rice with every meal and never be able to eat bread or eat bread with every meal and never be able to eat rice?

1031 WYR wake up tomorrow with a Marvel-style superpower or with Gandalf-style magical abilities?

1032 WYR settle for what you already know or keep on asking more questions?

1033 WYR live ten more years with excellent health or live thirty more years with declining health?

1034 WYR have a plan or fly by the seat of your pants?

1035 WYR choose a partner through looks or brains?

1036 WYR be left alone when you're feeling down or have someone cheer you up?

1037 WYR never be brokenhearted or never break someone's heart?

1038 WYR walk in the moonlight or run in the sun?

1039 WYR cry crocodile tears or cry wolf?

1040 WYR be where you are now or be anywhere other than where you are now?

1041 WYR be an honest simpleton or a dishonest genius?

1042 WYR super-sensitive taste or super-sensitive hearing?

1043 WYR learn the hard way or never make a mistake?

1044 WYR be a teacher of one thing or a student of many things?

1045 WYR do what you love or love what you're doing?

1046 WYR do your own thing or be in with the in-crowd?

1047 WYR sell all of your possessions or sell one of your organs?

1048 WYR relive yesterday just as it was or relive it to change it?

1049 WYR have greater responsibility or get rid of some of your responsibilities?

1050 WYR your shirts were two sizes too big or one size too small?

1051 WYR go it alone or have a sidekick?

1052 WYR watch less TV or spend less time online?

1053 WYR know when it's time to give in and let go or never quit?

1054 WYR believe nothing is impossible or believe there's no place like home?

1055 WYR believe only what you see or see whatever you put your mind to?

1056 WYR forget a memorable day or forfeit a valuable prize?

1057 WYR lose your mojo or lose your marbles?

1058 WYR burn rubber or have money to burn?

1059 WYR be more like your mom or more like your dad?

1060 WYR be able to remember every dream or forget every nightmare?

1061 WYR never experience loneliness or never have your trust broken?

1062 WYR go for the easy option or go for the luxury choice?

1063 WYR visit the Inventing Room in Willy Wonka's Chocolate Factory or the BFG's dream collection in his cave?

1064 WYR have hands that kept growing or feet that kept growing?

1065 WYR audition for *America's Got Talent* or *The Voice*?

1066 WYR swap lives with your favorite celebrity or a character from a book you've read?

1067 WYR buy things on impulse or write a shopping list and stick to it?

1068 WYR keep the name you have or permanently change your name?

1069 WYR only be able to watch reality TV shows on your TV or take part in one?

1070 WYR keep your own secret or keep a friend's secret for life?

1071 WYR be a male midwife or a female construction worker?

1072 WYR have an old banger that gets you around or save up until you can get a better car?

1073 WYR go back on your word or eat your words?

1074 WYR write someone a love letter or confess how you feel face to face?

1075 WYR believe in fate or believe that nothing happens unless you make it happen?

1076 WYR play hopscotch or make a cootie catcher?

1077 WYR never be able to smell your favorite scent again or never smell the aroma of your favorite food again?

1078 WYR never be hated or never be wrong?

1079 WYR have been born during World War I or during World War II?

1080 WYR have the sports car of your dreams or go on a road trip with your three best friends?

1081 WYR invite three celebrity guests or three historical figures to dinner?

1082 WYR only be able to listen to the music you loved ten years ago or watch the TV shows you loved ten years ago?

1083 WYR never be annoyed by anyone ever again or never lose your patience ever again?

1084 WYR be in a three-month lockdown situation with the smartest person you know or the funniest person you know?

1085 WYR learn how to home-cook your favorite restaurant meal or only have it once a year at a restaurant?

1086 WYR be rewarded for an act of heroism or for winning an international competition?

1087 WYR relive a year of your life or have no memories of a year in your life?

1088 WYR spend a day on a nude beach or have an embarrassing photo of you shared on social media?

1089 WYR eat the same foods at every meal for a month or eat at exactly the same mealtimes for a month?

1090 WYR live a movie moment or meet your favorite movie star?

1091 WYR be unpopular or be popular for doing something you're not proud of?

1092 WYR stick with tradition or never be governed by any tradition?

1093 WYR use your last wish to achieve a personal dream or to free the genie from the bottle?

1094 WYR have an audio recording of you singing in the shower or a video of you baking a cake shared on social media?

1095 WYR play a board game or a video game?

1096 WYR treat yourself by eating your favorite dessert or by buying a new item of clothing?

1097 WYR have an evening out at a comedy club or in a nightclub?

1098 WYR scuba dive or stage dive?

1099 WYR trip and fall as you step up to give a presentation or forget what you're saying halfway through a presentation?

1100 WYR become a millionaire or get to live in the fictional world of your favorite movie?

1101 WYR die in twenty years with no regrets or die in fifty with many regrets?

1102 WYR meet Taylor Swift or Bruce Springsteen?

1103 WYR hang out with Snoopy or Garfield?

1104 WYR relive your most embarrassing moment in life so far or give up the internet for six months?

1105 WYR hear voices in your head or see dead people?

1106 WYR eat cheese with live maggots or eat live sea urchin?

1107 WYR explore an underwater cave or an underground tunnel?

1108 WYR have no sense of humor or no sense of danger?

1109 WYR be agoraphobic or a germaphobe?

1110 WYR be a long-distance swimmer or a cross-country skier?

1111 WYR have the most beautiful eyes or the most amazing smile?

1112 WYR have a horrible job, but be able to retire comfortably in ten years or have your dream job, but work until you die?

1113 WYR have a job that starts at 4 am or one that starts at 4 pm?

1114 WYR be a garbage collector or a celebrity whom people love to hate?

1115 WYR know what the future holds for you or know what the future holds for your family members?

1116 WYR live a nomadic lifestyle or settle in one place?

1117 WYR have political power but be poor or be rich but have no political power?

1118 WYR spend a day as the person you are now but in the 1950s or in the 1970s?

1119 WYR party hard every night or never party again?

1120 WYR have a secret lair or a private jet?

1121 WYR have lunch with Warren Buffet or Madonna?

1122 WYR be covered in hair or be completely bald?

1123 WYR take early retirement or keep working on something until your dying day?

1124 WYR come back in another life as an energetic dog or a lazy cat?

1125 WYR never feel guilty again or never feel awkward again?

1126 WYR live in an area with slow internet or an unreliable cellphone signal?

1127 WYR answer your phone or let messages go to voicemail?

1128 WYR have bright lighting or soft lighting in your home if you could have only one?

1129 WYR be known by a catchphrase or a signature move?

1130 WYR never eat pizza again or never eat burgers again?

1131 WYR have a bad hair day or a gassy day?

1132 WYR have the power to wipe an annoying celebrity you can't stand from existence or a band?

1133 WYR be able to punch someone in the face and get away with it or pretend to be someone else and get away with it?

1134 WYR wish on a star or at a wishing well?

1135 WYR explore a new city on foot with a guide or take a bus tour around a city?

1136 WYR go on a hunting trip or go to a yoga retreat?

1137 WYR keep money you found in a taxi or give it to the taxi driver?

1138 WYR spend a gift of $5,000 on travel or on clothes and entertainment?

1139 WYR watch a horror movie on your own or watch a show you want to concentrate on with noisy friends?

1140 WYR it was the day after tomorrow or the day before yesterday?

1141 WYR be the person you are today or become a different version of you?

1142 WYR sleep an hour less than you need or go to bed an hour too early?

1143 WYR meet your doppelgänger or meet the doppelgänger of someone you know?

1144 WYR be a sleepwalker or a sleep talker?

1145 WYR do a dumpster dive or go metal detecting?

1146 WYR swallow gum or swallow a fly?

1147 WYR go for a swim immediately after a heavy meal or run with scissors in your hand?

1148 WYR be guilty of a traffic violation or of offending the fashion police on social media?

1149 WYR have your family turn into clowns or chimpanzees?

1150 WYR watch *Keeping Up with the Kardashians* or listen to Justin Bieber songs?

1151 WYR never make fun of someone ever again or never have others poke fun at you?

1152 WYR pursue a pie-in-the-sky idea or chase a red herring?

1153 WYR be able to do a one-handed handstand or a one-armed push-up?

1154 WYR bite your tongue or stub your toe?

1155 WYR fall asleep in the cinema or fall asleep on public transport?

1156 WYR be born rich in a poor country or be born into a royal family and a life of duty?

1157 WYR have your face on a $100 bill or be the face of an iconic brand?

1158 WYR go to sleep knowing there's a mosquito in the room or suspecting there may be a rat in the walls?

1159 WYR be the first line of defense or the last line?

1160 WYR be the voice of a lead character in an animated movie or have a bit part in a popular live-action movie?

1161 WYR have an alien friend or an invisible friend?

1162 WYR live in a windmill or a lighthouse?

1163 WYR have Rolanda Hooch or Pomona Sprout as your teacher?

1164 WYR walk on your toes in ballet shoes or wear fishermen's chest waders?

1165 WYR go on a date with Hannibal Lecter or Norman Bates?

1166 WYR stop to smell the flowers or be a rolling stone that gathers no moss?

1167 WYR have lunch with Neil Armstrong or Andy Warhol?

1168 WYR have your crime novel murderer dispose of the body in a shallow grave or by chopping it into pieces?

1169 WYR start every sentence with "As I was saying . . ." or end every sentence with ". . . don't you know"?

1170 WYR wear clashing colors or a jester's hat?

1171 WYR randomly scream at the top of your voice or randomly leap in the air once a day?

1172 WYR wear shoes that don't match your outfit or wear casual shoes with a formal outfit?

1173 WYR have your worst enemy read your diary or have all the pictures on your phone posted online?

1174 WYR have the feeling you're being followed or know you're being gossiped about?

1175 WYR never see your best friend again or never see your pet again?

1176 WYR empty the water from a swimming pool using a cup or count the grains of sand in a sandcastle?

1177 WYR have to flee a forest fire or a plague of locusts?

1178 WYR have bright orange knees or bright blue elbows?

1179 WYR eat a gallon of rocky road ice cream or an entire birthday cake in one sitting?

1180 WYR live in a cottage by a lake or in a houseboat on a lake?

1181 WYR have friends who are more attractive than you or who are smarter than you?

1182 WYR be the person who prevented a war or the person who ended a war?

1183 WYR have a weird laugh or a weird sense of humor?

1184 WYR have tentacles instead of arms or instead of legs?

1185 WYR have a round face or a square head?

1186 WYR have a hoverboard or inline skates?

1187 WYR have 1,000 people follow you on Instagram or $1,000?

1188 WYR have a gap between your front teeth or pointed ears?

1189 WYR be chased by an angry bee or an agitated seagull?

1190 WYR be sixteen forever or thirty-five forever?

1191 WYR have a house party or party in the park?

1192 WYR volunteer in an animal shelter or at a children's home?

1193 WYR never be able to watch football again or never be able to shoot hoops again?

1194 WYR drink a glass of vinegar or eat a block of butter?

1195 WYR never read a book again or never go bowling again?

1196 WYR switch bodies with the person on your right or switch heads with the person on your left?

1197 WYR be slapped across the face with a wet fish or licked on the face by a slobbery dog?

1198 WYR have no internet after 5 pm every day or only be able to send three text messages in a day?

1199 WYR only be able to receive telephone calls or only make calls and not receive them?

1200 WYR relax by sitting in a jacuzzi or by getting a massage?

1201 WYR be overweight or constantly under pressure?

1202 WYR be a champion waffle maker or a champion waffler?

1203 WYR have sand in your shoes or cookie crumbs in your bed?

1204 WYR only be able to wear purple for a month or only be able to eat white-colored foods for a week?

1205 WYR be a stock market trader or a flea market trader?

1206 WYR donate $5 to charity or take a chance on winning more by buying scratch-off cards?

1207 WYR wear a hat or a belt as your statement accessory?

1208 WYR eat birds to survive or eat bird seed to survive?

1209 WYR have been on board Apollo 13 or US Airways Flight 1549 (Miracle on the Hudson)?

1210 WYR be a cork bobbing on the ocean or a feather floating in the breeze?

1211 WYR pretend you're sick to get out of going somewhere or pretend to get a call to get out of a conversation?

1212 WYR drink tea from a cup and saucer or from a mug?

1213 WYR be out of your depth or out of time?

1214 WYR see a chimpanzee riding on a Segway or a monkey riding backwards on a pig?

1215 WYR have Indiana Jones's whip or Lara Croft's pistols?

1216 WYR it was raining tacos or hailing taquitos?

1217 WYR never get another haircut or never eat breakfast again?

1218 WYR your bedroom had the aroma of aged cheese or wet dog?

1219 WYR live in luxury in New York or in luxury in Los Angeles?

1220 WYR be lost in a cornfield or lost in a shopping mall?

1221 WYR take on an all-you-can-eat challenge or a hot-and-spicy food challenge?

1222 WYR live in a world with no evil people or a world with no disease?

1223 WYR be targeted by Pennywise or Chucky?

1224 WYR live without YouTube or without Netflix?

1225 WYR keep your finger on the pulse or let the world pass you by?

1226 WYR climb the corporate ladder or climb trees?

1227 WYR only have a shower at home or only have a bathtub at home?

1228 WYR learn how to dance the fandango or learn how to cook a soufflé?

1229 WYR have chocolate-flavored toothpaste or have chocolate sauce on fries?

1230 WYR play solitaire or blackjack?

1231 WYR have a lifetime supply of shampoo or breakfast cereal?

1232 WYR add a new word to the dictionary or discover a new planet?

1233 WYR read eBooks or listen to podcasts?

1234 WYR sleep with the AC on or with the windows open?

1235 WYR eat breakfast or lunch if you could eat only once a day?

1236 WYR have a career mentor or a life coach?

1237 WYR go to a family reunion or a school reunion?

1238 WYR have family you consider friends or friends you consider family?

1239 WYR direct a movie or star in a movie?

1240 WYR get it right the first time every time or be given a second chance every time?

1241 WYR read a newspaper or watch the news on TV?

1242 WYR take over the family business or start your own business?

1243 WYR be a cancer survivor or the lone survivor of a train wreck?

1244 WYR walk around a puddle or splash through a puddle?

1245 WYR drink iced coffee in the winter or hot chocolate in the summer?

1246 WYR win your height in books or your weight in gummy bears?

1247 WYR share a box of chicken nuggets with Usain Bolt or a pizza with Michael Phelps?

1248 WYR put peanut butter on jelly or jelly on peanut butter?

1249 WYR change something about yourself or change something about the world?

1250 WYR be able to have a conversation with your favorite stuffed animal or with people in paintings?

1251 WYR peel potatoes to feed 300 people or sort 600 socks into pairs?

1252 WYR have to wear wet clothes every day for a week or have dry lips for a month?

1253 WYR look at the stars in the night sky or listen to waves lapping on the shore?

1254 WYR be a master impersonator or a master ventriloquist?

1255 WYR be free as a bird or happy as a lark?

1256 WYR pretend to be into something you're not to impress someone or pretend not to like something you do?

1257 WYR help a loved one cover up a crime or give up your beloved pet if a loved one became allergic?

1258 WYR never look stupid or never take yourself too seriously?

1259 WYR be Doctor Who or Dr. Dolittle?

1260 WYR be right but resented by others or wrong and constantly reminded of it by others?

1261 WYR be lonely on your own or lonely in a crowd?

1262 WYR be a member of the Ghostbusters team or the X-Files team?

1263 WYR die a horrible death or eat a part of your body to survive?

1264 WYR be a cyborg or a Dalek?

1265 WYR be rich and mean or poor and kind?

1266 WYR live in a world with no electricity or no animals?

1267 WYR have $5 million that must be spent within five days or have $1 million to do with as you please in five years' time?

1268 WYR stick by the belief that honesty is the best policy or that nice guys finish last?

1269 WYR know all things or have some things in life remain a mystery?

1270 WYR become uglier as you age or dumber as you age?

1271 WYR share an apartment with a neat freak or a slob?

1272 WYR look better in photographs than you do in person or sound better on the phone than you do in person?

1273 WYR accidentally spit on someone's face when talking or drop your phone into a toilet?

1274 WYR stink or have everybody else stink except you?

1275 WYR have your parents embarrass you or be a disappointment to your parents?

1276 WYR listen to a ten-minute drum solo or a ten-minute banjo solo?

1277 WYR feel compelled to salute everyone you pass on the street or compelled to rap every time you speak?

1278 WYR be caught dancing in your underwear or caught licking your plate?

1279 WYR dance with someone who has no natural rhythm or sing with someone who is tone deaf?

1280 WYR have a friend who never pays their share or a friend who keeps asking to borrow money?

1281 WYR be told you're too serious or you're too ridiculous?

1282 WYR read a book containing poor grammar or one with a weak plotline?

1283 WYR be unable to say any words beginning with D or any words beginning with R?

1284 WYR have a night out with Miley Cyrus or Billie Ray Cyrus?

1285 WYR wear wrinkled clothes or dirty shoes?

1286 WYR maintain your ideal weight or always do what you say you're going to do?

1287 WYR everyone in the world suddenly became much younger than you or much older than you?

1288 WYR only be able to wear Crocs or only wear pajamas?

1289 WYR shoot hoops with Michael Jordan or play a round of golf with Tiger Woods?

1290 WYR have been at Woodstock in 1969 or Live Aid in 1985?

1291 WYR have free tickets to any baseball game for life or get paid $500,000 to never watch any baseball game ever again?

1292 WYR have your face in a painting or your body in a sculpture?

1293 WYR kiss a frog or be kissed by a monkey?

1294 WYR wake up in a *My Little Pony* world or a *Hunger Games* world?

1295 WYR own up to making a mistake or own up to telling a lie?

1296 WYR never have a headache again or never eat jellybeans again?

1297 WYR your eyes make the sound of camera shutters when you blink or sound like a steam train when you move?

1298 WYR win $1,000,000 or have your friend win $3,000,000?

1299 WYR be a zombie slayer or a tooth fairy?

1300 WYR burp bubbles or sneeze confetti?

1301 WYR be an Olympic athlete or a Hollywood actor?

1302 WYR have a day off like Ferris Bueller or an excellent adventure like Bill and Ted?

1303 WYR be hit with a frying pan, *Tom and Jerry*-style, or fall off cliffs, Wile E. Coyote-style?

1304 WYR be deaf or blind?

1305 WYR WYR be insane and know you're insane or insane and believe you're sane?

1306 WYR have been a passenger on the Hindenburg or on the Titanic?

1307 WYR have the A-Team come to your rescue or Charlie's Angels?

1308   WYR drive a fire truck or an ambulance?

1309   WYR have a lazy Susan on your table or a La-Z-Boy chair?

1310   WYR be able to crack your joints or lick your elbow?

1311   WYR travel at the speed of light or travel around the world in eighty days?

1312   WYR visit Area 51 or travel through the Bermuda Triangle?

1313   WYR bet everything you own on black or on red?

1314   WYR be featured on the front page of *The New York Times* or *Sports Illustrated*?

1315   WYR be in a globally famous band popular with kindergarten kids or be in an obscure rock band?

1316   WYR be able to see The Beatles in concert or the Ramones in concert?

1317   WYR dress like a rapper or dress like a rockabilly?

1318   WYR hire Knight Rider or Magnum, P.I. to fight in your corner?

1319   WYR have your house blown down by the big bad wolf or carried away by a twister?

1320   WYR have known Rosa Parks in the 1950s or Mahatma Gandhi in the 1920s?

1321   WYR stare daggers at someone or have an all-out shouting match?

1322   WYR live in a world without Velcro or a world without Post-It notes?

1323   WYR never be able to say "please" or never be able to say "thank you"?

1324   WYR be wanted or needed?

1325   WYR go hard or go home?

1326   WYR live in your car for a week or move in with an elderly aunt for a month?

1327   WYR be on trend or dare to be different and set your own style?

1328 WYR be trapped in a sandstorm or caught in quicksand?

1329 WYR get a part in a stage play or a TV soap opera?

1330 WYR listen to "Crazy Frog" or "Barbie Girl" on a loop?

1331 WYR wear the fashions of ancient Rome or Victorian London?

1332 WYR be a child star actor who fails as an adult actor or a one-hit wonder in the music industry?

1333 WYR never hear the sound of chalk squeaking on a blackboard again or the sound of slurping again?

1334 WYR be the audience warm-up guy or the fat lady who sings at the end?

1335 WYR be part of a firing squad or be a hangman?

1336 WYR have a stomachache or have a sore throat?

1337 WYR never have a dream come true or have your biggest dream *and* your worst nightmare come true?

1338 WYR learn how to read again or learn how to walk again?

1339 WYR visit a unicorn petting zoo or a dragon ride park?

1340 WYR spend a weekend with a paranoid person or someone who has just been dumped?

1341 WYR live for a year without money or without electricity?

1342 WYR have everything you touch turn to ice or turn to dust?

1343 WYR be a boy mistaken for a girl or a girl mistaken for a boy?

1344 WYR give up potatoes or pasta?

1345 WYR have all dogs try to attack you when they see you or all birds try to attack you when they see you?

1346 WYR be able to catch flies with your tongue like a frog or swivel your eyes like a chameleon?

1347 WYR have two left hands or two left feet?

1348 WYR slow down to walk with someone or have to jog to keep up with them?

1349 WYR go caving or mountain climbing?

1350 WYR pee your pants at a friend's party or pee in a swimming pool?

1351 WYR go on a protest march or start an online petition?

1352 WYR be in a relationship with someone ten years older or ten years younger than you?

1353 WYR break a bone or chip a tooth?

1354 WYR cut your own hair or have Edward Scissorhands cut your hair?

1355 WYR have a wardrobe malfunction or show up wearing the same outfit as someone else?

1356 WYR wear uncomfortable underwear or go commando?

1357 WYR live in a cave or live in a tree house?

1358 WYR be a hitchhiker or pick up a hitchhiker?

1359 WYR accidentally break an expensive item at a house party or throw up over the host?

1360 WYR be the person who gets seasick on a boat or be sitting next to the person who gets seasick?

1361 WYR never be fired from your job or never be questioned by a police officer?

1362 WYR use a gas station bathroom or pee on the side of the road?

1363 WYR blame a fart on a pet or an elderly relative in the room?

1364 WYR be nominated for an Oscar ten times and never win or win on your first nomination and never be nominated again?

1365 WYR be the only fairy that can't fly or the elf that's twice the size of the other elves?

1366 WYR be pranked with a whoopee cushion or with plastic wrap in the doorway?

1367 WYR have your phone ring at full volume in the cinema or in the library?

1368 WYR be a false alibi for a friend or let a friend be jailed for something they didn't do?

1369 WYR wear glasses all the time or contact lenses all the time?

1370 WYR get the highest score or make the longest word in a game of Scrabble?

1371 WYR dip fries into a milkshake or have bananas with pickle?

1372 WYR miss a high five or forget the punchline of the joke you're telling?

1373 WYR change a diaper or have a baby be sick on you?

1374 WYR lie in a job interview or use a fake ID?

1375 WYR be a vegetarian with a meat-eating partner or a meat-eater with a vegetarian partner?

1376 WYR be an amazing painter or a brilliant mathematician?

1377 WYR never lose your phone again or never lose your keys again?

1378 WYR disappoint a family member or a friend?

1379 WYR dye your hair and regret it or tell someone you love them and not mean it?

1380 WYR pick a wedgie in public or sneeze messily into your hand in public?

1381 WYR brush your teeth with a hairbrush or comb your hair with a fork?

1382 WYR see Taylor Swift or Eminem in concert?

1383 WYR have chapped lips that never heal or terrible dandruff that can't be treated?

1384 WYR be a survivor in a *Terminator* (computer uprising) world or *Dawn of the Dead* (zombie apocalypse) world?

1385 WYR have takeout on Tuesday or a family meal on Friday?

1386 WYR instantly change the color of your hair or the length of your hair?

1387 WYR have a *Star Trek*-style phaser or a *Men in Black*-style neuralyzer?

1388 WYR crawl everywhere or butt shuffle everywhere?

1389 WYR be a guitar-smashing rock star or smash your computer with a baseball bat for real?

1390 WYR have a car with a top speed of 30 mph or be able to run at 40 mph with endless endurance?

1391 WYR have been the first person to reach the North Pole or the first person to climb Mount Everest?

1392 WYR have skin like a coconut shell or skin like a pineapple?

1393 WYR live in Downton Abbey or Winterfell Castle (*Game of Thrones*)?

1394 WYR be caught kissing your reflection or kissing a photo of a celebrity?

1395 WYR never be in a car accident or never be in handcuffs?

1396 WYR steal pens from work or steal candy from a kid?

1397 WYR miss a deadline or miss a payment?

1398 WYR get up early to get a job done or stay up late to get a job done?

1399 WYR vomit in a taxi or pee your pants in a taxi?

1400 WYR know when you're going to die or how you're going to die?

1401 WYR have unlimited sushi for life or unlimited tacos for life?

1402 WYR accidentally break a piece of furniture by sitting on it or accidentally break a window?

1403 WYR be shouted at by a customer or by your boss?

1404 WYR break up with someone in public or have someone break up with you by text?

1405 WYR talk to yourself or talk to Alexa (Siri)?

1406 WYR be able to shed your skin like a snake or regrow a missing limb like a salamander?

1407 WYR share a water bottle with three friends or share a dip with a double dipper?

1408 WYR find a hair in your food or a fly in your drink?

1409 WYR be blown over by the wind or knocked off your feet by a wave?

1410 WYR rock out to Green Day or bop to Katy Perry?

1411 WYR never get a speeding ticket or never get carded?

1412 WYR have one nipple or two belly buttons?

1413 WYR get something stuck up your nose or in your ear?

1414 WYR meet a mermaid or an elf?

1415 WYR have been picked for the school's sports team or picked for the lead in the school musical?

1416 WYR regret a haircut or regret a piercing?

1417 WYR do a tandem bungee jump or a tandem skydive?

1418 WYR dance on a table or slide down a bannister?

1419 WYR know how to milk a cow or lasso a calf?

1420 WYR not be able to see any colors or have mild but constant tinnitus (ringing in the ears)?

1421 WYR have constantly dry eyes or a constant runny nose?

1422 WYR spend all day sitting or standing?

1423 WYR listen to Johnny Cash or Johnny Rotten of the Sex Pistols?

1424 WYR know the history of every object you touched or be able to talk to animals?

1425 WYR travel Route 66 on a Harley-Davidson or in a Ford Mustang?

1426 WYR have a week-long vacation in Ireland or a long weekend in Hong Kong?

1427 WYR work on a production line or work in research?

1428 WYR be kept alive for years on life support or be allowed to die?

1429 WYR be forced to eat only spicy food or only incredibly bland food?

1430 WYR sleep in the nude or sleep without bed linen?

1431 WYR have a life-changing adventure or be able to stop time?

1432 WYR travel first class and stay in a budget hotel or travel budget class and stay in a five-star hotel?

1433 WYR be responsible for the death of a child or for the deaths of three adults?

1434 WYR have a pet jellyfish or a pet stick insect?

1435 WYR be twelve inches tall or twelve feet tall?

1436 WYR meet the author of your favorite book or be able to meet a character from the book?

1437 WYR go to jail for four years for something you didn't do or get away with something you did but live in fear of being caught?

1438 WYR play video games for twelve hours nonstop or watch movies for twelve hours nonstop?

1439 WYR only ever have one hairstyle and no bad hair days or have the option to try lots of different styles?

1440 WYR never be sweaty again or never get dirty again?

1441 WYR get free tickets to a theme park or a water park?

1442 WYR be a Minion or an Oompa-Loompa?

1443 WYR be an extra in an Oscar-winning movie or the lead in a box office bomb?

1444 WYR have a crooked nose from a sports injury or a cauliflower ear?

1445 WYR cook a meal blindfolded or eat a meal with your hands tied behind your back?

1446 WYR army crawl everywhere or log roll everywhere?

1447 WYR tie your shoelaces wearing mittens or send a text using only your nose?

1448 WYR be able to balance a spoon on the end of your nose or touch your nose with your tongue?

1449 WYR be able to talk to and understand cats or dogs?

1450 WYR be a skilled seamstress/tailor or have "a very particular set of skills" like Liam Neeson in *Taken*?

1451 WYR win a staring contest or an arm-wrestling match?

1452 WYR be known as the life and soul of the party or the go-to person in an emergency?

1453 WYR always be overdressed or always underdressed?

1454 WYR be prone to dropping things or prone to forgetting things?

1455 WYR be known by one name (mononymous) or have a hyphenated last name?

1456 WYR get an animal-image tattoo or have a tattoo of someone's name?

1457 WYR take part in the "mannequin challenge" or the "ice bucket challenge"?

1458 WYR have a secret family recipe or a family heirloom?

1459 WYR have $25,000 in gold or in bitcoin?

1460 WYR have seven sons or seven daughters?

1461 WYR have a ninety percent chance of winning $90,000 or a fifty percent chance of winning $50 million?

1462 WYR own three homes or have $300,000 in the bank?

1463 WYR be in a *War of the Worlds* world or a *Walking Dead* world?

1464 WYR be immune to physical pain or have no emotions?

1465 WYR be a logical thinker or be considered a bit of a space cadet?

1466 WYR be lucky in love or talented in your career?

1467 WYR be famous for pulling off an audacious heist or a daring jailbreak?

1468 WYR be the record producer who turned down The Beatles or the publisher who rejected J.K. Rowling?

1469 WYR be the second choice of your first love or be the first choice of your second love?

1470 WYR be assimilated into the Borg (*Star Trek*) or have your brain transplanted into an animal form (Rocket Raccoon)?

1471 WYR cheat death or cheat on a partner?

1472 WYR socialize with mega-rich entrepreneurs or famous musicians?

1473 WYR love your face but not your body or love your body but not your face?

1474 WYR be the defense attorney for a guilty person or the prosecution against an innocent person?

1475 WYR share an office with a narcissist or a sociopath?

1476 WYR be malnourished or dehydrated?

1477 WYR have Morgan Freeman or Patrick Stewart narrate your life story?

1478 WYR be transported into the world of Oliver Twist or the world of Huckleberry Finn?

1479 WYR defend yourself with an electric hand whisk or a waffle iron?

1480 WYR wipe Valentine's Day or Groundhog Day from the calendar?

1481 WYR hire a sixteen-year-old babysitter or a seventy-six-year-old babysitter?

1482 WYR live in a small apartment that's a five-minute walk from your workplace or a big house that's a thirty-minute drive away?

1483 WYR have been twenty-one in 1969 or twenty-one in 1989?

1484 WYR spend time doing it yourself to save money or spend money on having someone else do it to save time?

1485 WYR choose truth or dare?

1486 WYR take the blame to get your best friend out of trouble or take credit for something to get your worst enemy into trouble?

1487 WYR only be able to see one color or smell one smell?

1488 WYR hear a growl behind you or a scream ahead of you when you're alone in the woods?

1489 WYR have the power to cause chaos by transporting a furious elephant into any moment in history or by transporting a modern gadget?

1490 WYR be able to change your name or choose your own nickname?

1491 WYR be able to live someone else's life for fifteen minutes or read someone's thoughts for fifteen minutes?

1492 WYR own a cat with a human face or a dog with human hands for paws?

1493 WYR be tasked with redesigning your country's national flag or rewriting its national anthem?

1494 WYR have a fear of a duck watching you (anatidaephobia) or fear of the color yellow (xanthophobia)?

1495 WYR be able to revive plants with your tears or kill weeds with your laughter?

1496 WYR be armed with a banjo or an egg whisk in a zombie attack?

1497 WYR be stranded on an island like Tom Hanks in *Castaway* or stranded on Mars like Matt Damon in *The Martian*?

1498 WYR be caught dancing with a mop or singing with a banana microphone?

1499 WYR work behind the scenes at The White House or work behind the scenes in Hollywood?

1500 WYR be able to custom-make your ideal partner or your ideal family?

1501 WYR hear the ground complaining when you walk on it or your car complaining when you drive badly?

1502 WYR animals walked upright for a day or humans walked on all-fours for a day?

1503 WYR have freckles on your nose or a dimple on your chin?

1504 WYR be accused of being a spendthrift or a miser?

1505 WYR laugh like a hyena or sound like a donkey when you laugh?

1506 WYR meet a dinosaur or an alien?

1507 WYR never get lost or never lose your balance?

1508 WYR reveal your deepest fear or your secret crush?

1509 WYR lick the floor or lick food retrieved from a trash can?

1510 WYR be the opposite sex for a month or work the night shift for a month?

1511 WYR be caught sucking your thumb or sleeping with a stuffed toy?

1512 WYR hurt someone by telling a lie or by saying something mean?

1513 WYR keep a smile on your face all day or get through a day without laughing?

1514 WYR never lose your memory or never lose your eyesight?

1515 WYR have your most disgusting (and secret) habit discovered or be arrested by police and taken in for questioning?

1516 WYR hold a live insect in your mouth for ten seconds or have rats walk over you for ten seconds?

1517 WYR never feel envy again or never feel vengeful again?

1518 WYR find a skunk in your bed or a goose in your shower?

1519 WYR switch socks with the person on your left or switch tops with the person on your right?

1520 WYR have all your clothes fit perfectly or have the most comfortable pillow, blankets, and sheets in existence?

1521 WYR take part in a twenty-four-hour dance-a-thon or a twenty-four-hour cook-a-thon?

1522 WYR be considered vain or plain?

1523 WYR put relationships over career or put your career first?

1524 WYR be considered aggressive or a pushover?

1525 WYR know how to pick a lock or how to hotwire a car?

1526 WYR feel free or safe?

1527 WYR be a member of your favorite band for a day or be transported into your favorite game for a day?

1528 WYR have nine lives like a cat or live the life of Riley?

1529 WYR never be able to talk to anyone again or never be able to touch anyone again?

1530 WYR work in waste disposal or bomb disposal?

1531 WYR slip and fall in a puddle of vomit or get sprayed by a skunk?

1532 WYR live a hermit's life or be the life and soul of every party?

1533 WYR have telescopic legs like Inspector Gadget or extendable arms like Mr. Tickle?

1534 WYR see the creation of the universe or the end of the universe?

1535 WYR lack imagination or lack subtlety?

1536 WYR eat a handful of hair or drink a cup of spit?

1537 WYR only be able to eat green vegetables or red fruit?

1538 WYR be prepared like a Boy Scout or be prepared to wing it?

1539 WYR eat only pizza for a year or eat no pizza for a year?

1540 WYR be able to clear the world's oceans of plastic or save the rainforests?

1541 WYR live with a dog that snores loudly or a partner who talks in their sleep?

1542 WYR lose a day of your life every time you swear or every time you say something mean?

1543 WYR hang out with the first person you ever had a crush on or the first person you ever dated?

1544 WYR be proactive or procrastinate?

1545 WYR wear the fashions your parents wore as teenagers or the fashions your grandparents wore?

1546 WYR be able to do a split or do a backflip?

1547 WYR have free internet for life or free food for life?

1548 WYR give a colleague a piggyback around your workplace for a day or be given piggybacks all day?

1549 WYR eat a banana without peeling it or swallow gum?

1550 WYR be a skilled whistler or a skilled spoons player?

1551 WYR have bad breath or smelly feet?

1552 WYR have eyes that can film everything or ears that can record all sound?

1553 WYR paint a picture or paint a garden fence?

1554 WYR switch places with a spider or a mouse?

1555 WYR have three eyes or a tail?

1556 WYR be trapped in a room with walls moving in or tied to a post with water levels rising?

1557 WYR wake up to a snake or a bear in your bedroom?

1558 WYR have your car written off in a car crash or lose all your files in a computer crash?

1559 WYR find $50 or be hugged?

1560 WYR live in a country with a low cost of living but horrible weather or live in a country with a high cost of living and amazing weather?

1561 WYR be a world-renowned photographer or a world-renowned animal trainer?

1562 WYR feel brave or feel smart?

1563 WYR share everything in your life with others or keep it all to yourself?

1564 WYR understand how animals communicate or the laws of quantum mechanics?

1565 WYR be able to successfully grow anything you want in the yard or be an accomplished classical musician?

1566 WYR be a passenger in Toad of Toad Hall's motorcar (*The Wind in the Willows*) or Cruella de Vil's car (*101 Dalmatians*)?

1567 WYR know the muffin man or know the way to San Jose?

1568 WYR tell a stranger their underwear was showing or look the other way?

1569 WYR fix the hole in the ozone layer or save the Great Barrier Reef?

1570 WYR have money and no love or love and no money?

1571 WYR have great wisdom or good health?

1572 WYR marry a poor person from your culture or a rich person from a different culture?

1573 WYR be able to touch your toes without bending your knees or rub your tummy and pat your head?

1574 WYR have no nose or no ears?

1575 WYR be woken up by an air horn every morning or do a four-mile run on waking every morning?

1576 WYR meet a mini hippo or a giant wasp?

1577 WYR be the apple of someone's eye or be someone with a finger in every pie?

1578 WYR live in the world as it is today or live in the world as it was a hundred years ago?

1579 WYR work alone in the day or work with colleagues on the night shift?

1580 WYR ask a loaded question or shoot from the hip when answering a question?

1581 WYR let sleeping dogs lie or let the cat out of the bag?

1582 WYR drink warm soda or eat cold curry?

1583 WYR be a skilled architect or a skilled graphic designer?

1584 WYR go gray naturally as you age or dye your hair to cover gray as you age?

1585 WYR visit a book festival or an art festival?

1586 WYR go ghost hunting or storm chasing?

1587 WYR never have less than fifty percent charge on your phone or always have $50 in your pocket?

1588 WYR have super-sharp reflexes or be super flexible?

1589 WYR wear entirely neon pink or entirely plaid?

1590 WYR have whatever you are thinking to appear above your head for everyone to see or have absolutely everything you do livestreamed for anyone to see?

1591 WYR be hated or be a hater?

1592 WYR be in a long-distance relationship or be married to someone in the military?

1593 WYR be rich and famous or just rich?

1594 WYR be sophisticated and aloof or be the boy/girl next door and gregarious?

1595 WYR learn to communicate using Morse code or semaphore flag signals?

1596 WYR eat green apples or red grapes?

1597 WYR go without your phone or go without food for two days?

1598 WYR have lunch with a friend or dinner with colleagues?

1599 WYR be the child of celebrity parents or have a famous sibling?

1600 WYR be born into a family that's feared (like Corleone) or have a sibling who is on death row?

1601 WYR have a DJ or a live band at your party?

1602 WYR lose your heart to a starship trooper or leave your heart in San Francisco?

1603 WYR be a legendary adventurer or a legendary performer?

1604 WYR go sugar-free or gluten-free?

1605 WYR stay in bed all day or stay awake all night?

1606 WYR move to a new city or town every week or never be able to leave the city or town you were born in?

1607 WYR camp for a night with a stranger or camp for a night alone?

1608 WYR work for an angry boss or work in an environment that makes you angry?

1609 WYR save an antique painting or your favorite shoes from a fire?

1610 WYR be able to undo every mistake you ever made or never make another mistake going forward?

1611 WYR have charisma or great hair?

1612 WYR be alone on Valentine's Day or alone on New Year's Eve?

1613 WYR have a cut on your lip or a canker sore on your tongue?

1614 WYR be blackmailed or wear chain mail?

1615 WYR have a parrot that talks all day or a cat that yowls at night?

1616 WYR be held hostage for six months or go into hiding for six months?

1617 WYR be surrounded by people who brag nonstop about their great life or people who moan nonstop about their unfair life?

1618 WYR do an outdoor job in pouring rain or under a baking hot sun?

1619 WYR pull out one of your own teeth or stitch up your own arm?

1620 WYR lose all the photographs you've taken this year or all the photographs of you in your childhood?

1621 WYR have four arms or two mouths?

1622 WYR be able to wash yourself like a cat or dry yourself like a dog?

1623 WYR share a cab with someone who has bad breath or someone with body odor?

1624 WYR meet the real Easter bunny or the real Santa?

1625 WYR be able to read lips or know sign language?

1626 WYR fall out of bed or fall off a bench?

1627 WYR end racism or end sexism?

1628 WYR plunge into ice-cold water or chug a glass of ice-cold water?

1629 WYR lose the last piece of your 2,000-piece jigsaw or lose a card from your deck?

1630 WYR spend a night in the hospital or in jail?

1631 WYR never play your favorite sport again or lose whenever you play?

1632 WYR be as sly as a fox or as gentle as a lamb?

1633 WYR be blocked by someone on social media or be ghosted?

1634 WYR break the law or break both your arms?

1635 WYR cry for no reason or laugh for no reason?

1636 WYR be a hip-hop superstar or hula hoop superstar?

1637 WYR have met Anne Frank or Victor Frankenstein?

1638 WYR have an overly possessive partner or an overly needy pet?

1639 WYR be a roofer with a fear of heights or a coal miner with a fear of small spaces?

1640 WYR have a romantic dinner or a romantic slow dance?

1641 WYR be transported into a medieval banquet or a Roman feast?

1642 WYR have a traditional wedding or get married in Las Vegas?

1643 WYR only need to sleep for one night each week or only need to eat one meal each week?

1644 WYR be able to complete a one-week project in one day or complete two one-week projects in one week?

1645 WYR be a bounty hunter or a bargain hunter?

1646 WYR wear a neck brace for a month or have braces on your teeth for two months?

1647 WYR be on the outside looking in or be an outlier?

1648 WYR only be able to read the first half of any book or watch the second half of any movie?

1649 WYR ask a question no one wants to answer or give an answer no one wants to hear?

1650 WYR decorate your home all in red or wear only red?

1651 WYR be able to change the way your hair parts or change the shape of your eyebrows at will?

1652 WYR your hair turned green in direct sunlight or your skin turned green when wet?

1653 WYR have a job on an assembly line or a supermarket checkout?

1654 WYR be able to change the length of your hair by pushing your belly button or have a prehensile ponytail?

1655 WYR eat meatloaf or go to a Meatloaf concert?

1656 WYR be chased by hyenas or hippos?

1657 WYR be on a long bus journey with twenty Elvis impersonators or twenty mime artists?

1658 WYR settle an argument with a break-dancing contest or a bake-off?

1659 WYR be able to adjust your height by twiddling your earlobe or change your hairstyle by pushing your nose?

1660 WYR have paws instead of hands or hooves instead of feet?

1661 WYR sleep hanging upside down like a bat or sleep standing up like a giraffe?

1662 WYR feel compelled to follow everything you say with an evil laugh or begin every sentence with "Simon says . . ."?

1663 WYR tell people you come from a galaxy far, far away or you come from a land that time forgot?

1664 WYR be stuck on a desert island with a basketball or a Rubik's Cube?

1665 WYR have an extreme phobia of trees and flowers or of people named after trees and flowers?

1666 WYR have your strength determined by the length of your hair or your intelligence by the length of your fingers?

1667 WYR be able to play your fingers like panpipes or your thighs like bongos?

1668 WYR sneeze uncontrollably every time you see a cat or itch uncontrollably every time you see a dog?

1669 WYR wear a Carmen Miranda-style fruit hat or a Lady Gaga-inspired meat outfit to work?

1670 WYR have an interchangeable Lego head or be Mr. Potato Head?

1671 WYR be able to choose the weather each day or choose how many hours you spend at work each day?

1672 WYR be able to style your hair by thinking about it or wash and dry your clothes by dancing around them?

1673 WYR have Captain Kirk or Captain Han Solo on your tag team?

1674 WYR be the author of *101 Things to Do with a Stick* or *101 Meals to Make with Kale*?

1675 WYR win the Nobel Prize in Physics or be a noble knight with a trusty steed?

1676 WYR be locked overnight in a museum or an amusement park?

1677 WYR be tasked with finding a needle in a haystack or finding a white cat in a snowstorm?

1678 WYR be a storm in a teacup or be the eye of a storm?

1679 WYR enter an Elvis impersonator contest or the rock-paper-scissors world championships?

1680 WYR have three wheels on your wagon or be three sheets to the wind?

1681 WYR forget where you parked your car or accidently get into the wrong car?

1682 WYR be one person's favorite person or be a fan favorite?

1683 WYR yodel to save your life or tap dance to save your life?

1684 WYR listen to the sound of a breeze in the trees or bacon sizzling?

1685 WYR have your eye on the prize or play it by ear?

1686 WYR win the lottery and die the next day or get a free ride when you've already paid?

1687 WYR spend a rainy afternoon playing Uno with family or playing *Animal Crossing* alone?

1688 WYR re-read a book or re-watch a movie?

1689 WYR only be able to wash your hair three times a year or check your phone three times a week?

1690 WYR be the President of the United States for a day or a billionaire for a day?

1691 WYR hold your horses or be like a bat out of hell?

1692 WYR look like a model but sound like Chewbacca or look like Chewbacca but sound like Donny and Marie?

1693 WYR have your face suddenly become pixelated or your voice suddenly become disguised on a first date?

1694 WYR watch lambs skipping in a meadow or fish jumping in a pond?

1695 WYR be an Englishman in New York or a New Yorker in London?

1696 WYR be accused of being too optimistic or too pessimistic?

1697 WYR have a permanent itch on your nose or a permanently sweaty left foot?

1698 WYR be Zoom-bombed during an important video conference or be unable to turn off the cat-face filter?

1699 WYR only listen to sad songs or not listen to music at all?

1700 WYR be able to buy top-ups for emotions or buy upgrades for broken hearts?

1701 WYR use popular catchphrases from TV shows or create your own?

1702 WYR have barely legible handwriting but great typing skills or have beautiful handwriting and only be able to type with two fingers?

1703 WYR take a quick shower or a long bath?

1704 WYR always wear socks or never wear socks?

1705 WYR have all your debt canceled or be free from all allergies?

1706 WYR see a biographical movie of your favorite singer or read your favorite actor's autobiography?

1707 WYR stick with your favorite brand or get paid to give your opinion on new brands?

1708 WYR only own the few things you need or own lots of things even if you never use them?

1709 WYR never lose anything again or never lose your temper?

1710 WYR be able to wiggle your ears or curl your tongue?

1711 WYR go dancing for a night in the 1950s or the 1970s?

1712 WYR be able to shrink your car to pocketsize when you're not driving or supersize yourself at will?

1713 WYR do the job you do now or be able to snap your fingers and have the skills you need to change jobs?

1714 WYR trade places with a person or an animal?

1715 WYR be able to ask your past self a single question or ask your future self a single question?

1716 WYR be a talented liar or a talented lie detector?

1717 WYR be a bookworm or go on a wormhole adventure?

1718 WYR live in virtual reality where you are all-powerful or live in the real world and be able to go anywhere but not be able to interact with anyone or anything?

1719 WYR write a book or be the subject of a book?

1720 WYR look the same at forty as you did at twenty or look the same at eighty as you did at forty?

1721 WYR have someone tell you that you're smart or you're funny?

1722 WYR have eyebrows that can crawl around your face or hair that can fly away at random intervals?

1723 WYR take a daily bath with a friendly hippo or go for a daily jog with a friendly emu?

1724 WYR have "Stayin' Alive" play at your funeral or "D-I-V-O-R-C-E" play at your wedding?

1725 WYR accidentally sit on fast-acting Gorilla Glue or wake up in the gorilla enclosure at the zoo?

1726 WYR cry every time you laugh or fart every time you sneeze?

1727 WYR be in the crow's nest on a ship in a sea storm or in an elevator when an earthquake strikes?

1728 WYR ban fake tanning products or guyliner (eyeliner for men)?

1729 WYR look down your nose or put your foot in your mouth?

1730 WYR eat food through your fingertips or breathe through your elbows?

1731 WYR listen to "sounds of the sixties" or "sounds of the seventies" on the radio?

1732 WYR see feelings or feel sounds?

1733 WYR follow the instructions or throw caution to the wind?

1734 WYR be a high diver who forgets how to swim or a racing driver who forgets how to drive?

1735 WYR be able to give change for a dollar by putting it in your mouth or be able to breathe fire?

1736 WYR have a bird in the hand or two in the bush?

1737 WYR have six fingers on your left hand or three fingers on your right hand?

1738 WYR use mustard instead of hair gel or salad dressing instead of shower gel?

1739 WYR go on a voyage with Sinbad the Sailor or Jason and the Argonauts?

1740 WYR live in a world where nose-thumbing has replaced handshakes or the "whatever" forehead gesture has replaced "hello"?

1741 WYR live the next 10 years of your life in China or India?

1742 WYR live in a world where there is no poverty and no TV or no hunger and no fast food?

1743 WYR it only ever rained at night or only ever snowed in January?

1744 WYR be able to play guitar like Jimi Hendrix or write songs like Bob Dylan?

1745 WYR have the final say on who gets to star in movies or have control over who wins sporting championships?

1746 WYR eat to live or live to eat?

1747 WYR be a master at the art of origami or macramé?

1748 WYR go bowling with Fred Flintstone or Uncle Buck?

1749 WYR feel compelled to tango every time you hear a car horn or shout "Olé!" every time you cross a street?

1750 WYR be caught telling a lie in the town of Embarrass, Minnesota or the town of Truth or Consequences in New Mexico?

1751 WYR live in a different town in the state you're in now or live in a different state?

1752 WYR inherit personality traits from your parents or your grandparents?

1753 WYR have a permanent Snapchat filter on your face or have the "bloopers" of your daily life appear on YouTube?

1754 WYR be "Lost in the Supermarket" or "Lost in Space"?

1755 WYR have a magical compass that can lead you to anywhere you want to go or one that can lead you to whatever you want to find?

1756 WYR play for the Dallas Dolphins or the Miami Cowboys?

1757 WYR be a one-eared rabbit or a one-eyed mouse?

1758 WYR travel the world for a year with all expenses paid or have $500,000 to spend on whatever you want?

1759 WYR step barefoot on a sea urchin or grab a thistle with bare hands?

1760 WYR scale a poodle or a pangolin up to the size of a horse?

1761 WYR have a perfect day or a perfect evening?

1762 WYR be late for a meeting at work or late the first time you meet your partner's parents?

1763 WYR have the world's biggest collection of sports memorabilia or army tanks?

1764 WYR have the job of winding up the clocks in a clock museum or cleaning the mirrors in a hall of mirrors?

1765 WYR break the world record for most CDs balanced on one finger or most socks put on one foot in one minute?

1766 WYR be in prison for a year or be in a coma for a year?

1767 WYR listen to all 154 of Shakespeare's sonnets or "Crazy Frog" on a loop?

1768 WYR live in a world without mashed potatoes or a world without pumpkin pie?

1769 WYR be like a fish out of water or be in hot water?

1770 WYR face your biggest fear for $1 million or do a picked-at-random dare for $2 million?

1771 WYR be able to control fire or water?

1772 WYR be a sight for sore eyes or catch someone's eye?

1773 WYR be caught in an unexpected location or caught doing something surprising?

1774 WYR make one gargantuan decision right now or make one big decision every year with a coin toss?

1775 WYR offer a friend career advice or personal advice?

1776 WYR see the first artist you saw in concert again or the last artist you saw in concert?

1777 WYR play two truths and a lie or charades?

1778 WYR be able to go back and change something your parents did or go back and change something you said to your parents?

1779 WYR get a tattoo of the pet you dreamed of having when you were five or of the person on your left?

1780 WYR be able to erase a year in your life (unlive it) or erase three people (unmeet them)?

1781 WYR relive the best party you ever went to or the best family outing you ever went on?

1782 WYR be tested on your spelling ability right now or your math ability right now?

1783 WYR be able to buy one object, no matter the price, or meet one person (dead or alive)?

1784 WYR be able to choose the gender of your unborn baby or their physical features?

1785 WYR have written a play or had an article published in a magazine?

1786 WYR take ballet lessons to become more graceful or take up rowing to improve your stamina?

1787 WYR not be able to swim or not be able to ride a bicycle?

1788 WYR be able to hold your breath for two minutes or run a mile in under seven minutes?

1789 WYR only eat raw potato or only ever eat cooked (never raw) tomatoes?

1790 WYR only cook once each week or only cook with a deep fryer?

1791 WYR drizzle honey or sprinkle cilantro on all food?

1792 WYR have a pet peacock or visit Bangkok?

1793 WYR pay with the exact change or never have anything smaller than a $20 bill?

1794 WYR not be able to whistle or not be able to snap your fingers?

1795 WYR meet Tom Cruise or go on a river cruise?

1796 WYR be tired no matter how much you sleep or constantly hungry no matter how much you eat?

1797 WYR never use a public restroom or never give a speech in public?

1798 WYR take part in a murder mystery weekend or ride in the Mystery Machine with Scooby-Doo?

1799 WYR visit Disneyland on your own or eat out at a restaurant on your own?

1800 WYR spend fifteen minutes trying to catch a fly or spend fifteen minutes on hold on the phone?

1801 WYR play the harmonica or sing acapella?

1802 WYR take part in a mud wrestling contest or make a Mississippi mud pie?

1803 WYR go ice fishing or learn how to make ice sculptures?

1804 WYR always go to bed before 10 pm or always eat chocolate chip pancakes for breakfast?

1805 WYR WYR spend two years with your soulmate before they die, leaving you to never love again, or spend your life with someone nice you settled for?

1806 WYR never break a bone or never break a promise?

1807 WYR be able to play a guitar with your teeth or behind your back?

1808 WYR be able to touch your nose with your tongue or play the flute with your nose?

1809 WYR have a fear of anything that jumps or anything that beeps?

1810 WYR never get divorced or never meet your soulmate?

1811 WYR your spirit animal was an inchworm or a dung beetle?

1812 WYR dance a polka every day at noon for a week or wear only polka dot clothing for a week?

1813 WYR eat the world's stinkiest cheese or down a whole jar of pickles in one sitting?

1814 WYR be a member of the fashion police or the grammar police?

1815 WYR know how to fix cars or how to outfox the opposition?

1816 WYR never be too old to laugh when ketchup makes a fart sound or be old enough to know better?

1817 WYR have a TV in every room in your house or have a room in your house just for shoes?

1818 WYR stick by the golden rule or have a golden goose?

1819 WYR be able to reverse one decision every day or be able to pause time for a minute every day?

1820 WYR have a blast or get a blast from the past?

1821 WYR have a fear of buttons or feel compelled to push all buttons (especially big red ones)?

1822 WYR carry the Olympic torch or be the Human Torch?

1823 WYR eat a spoonful of wasabi or a spoonful of Tabasco sauce?

1824 WYR be the life and soul of the party but secretly feel depressed or have people think you're boring while you're really content with life?

1825 WYR have your ducks in a row or duck and dive?

1826 WYR be a driving instructor or a diving instructor?

1827 WYR be addicted to eating dirt or eating soap?

1828 WYR be a straight-A student or a member of the A-Team?

1829 WYR have a fear of water or be addicted to eating ice?

1830 WYR always use the rule of thumb or have a green thumb?

1831 WYR make it law that children should be seen and not heard or people over the age of seventy-five shouldn't drive?

1832 WYR be taller than your parents or have your children be taller than you?

1833 WYR be under someone's thumb or stand out like a sore thumb?

1834 WYR play by the rules or bend the rules?

1835 WYR be dressed to the nines or go the whole nine yards?

1836 WYR be the underdog or a dark horse?

1837 WYR not know how to cook or not know how to drive?

1838 WYR lose all your teeth or all your hair?

1839 WYR be only able to whisper or only able to shout?

1840 WYR never gain weight or never get sick?

1841 WYR prepare a Thanksgiving meal for twelve people or give a speech in front of 112 people?

1842 WYR own thirty pairs of socks or thirty hats?

1843 WYR be able to swim like the Man from Atlantis or run like The Six Million Dollar Man?

1844 WYR find your dream job or true love?

1845 WYR be ten years older than your sibling or ten years younger?

1846 WYR be someone's rock or rock the boat?

1847 WYR be a stand-up comedian or a one-man band?

1848 WYR never own a house or never own a car?

1849 WYR kiss a crocodile or tickle a bear?

1850 WYR be a cheesemaker or a winemaker?

1851 WYR watch *The Sound of Music* or *The Great Escape*?

1852 WYR be an art freak or be a freakshow on the dance floor?

1853 WYR be a city slicker or a country bumpkin?

1854 WYR be the hider or the seeker in a game of hide and seek?

1855 WYR walk the talk or walk the line?

1856 WYR share a loveseat with a smelly cat or a bed with a gassy dog?

1857 WYR be shy or work-shy?

1858 WYR read the book or watch the movie?

1859 WYR never marry or never have children?

1860 WYR your pet lived twice as long as normal or was twice as intelligent as normal?

1861 WYR have your pride hurt or have to swallow your pride?

1862 WYR never remember someone's face or always forget their name?

1863 WYR be sitting on a gold mine or be worth your weight in gold?

1864 WYR be weird and wacky or shrewd and sagacious?

1865 WYR stop doing something you do daily or start doing something new on top of what you do daily?

1866 WYR have to run to save your life or eat food out of a trash can to survive?

1867 WYR daydream about things you've done or things you'd like to do?

1868 WYR clean rest stop toilets or a slaughterhouse for a living?

1869 WYR visit the land of the rising sun or the land of milk and honey?

1870 WYR be able to grow at will or be able to shrink at will?

1871 WYR hear the sound of silence or the sound of children playing?

1872 WYR have no eyebrows or no eyelashes?

1873 WYR snicker like Muttley or giggle like Elmo?

1874 WYR be able to see what is behind every door or be able to open all doors by saying "Open sesame!"?

1875 WYR have a job that pays $100 an hour but lets you work from home or a job that pays $180 an hour but requires you to be physically present?

1876 WYR be as good as gold or be born with a silver spoon in your mouth?

1877 WYR have the odds stacked against you or be the odd one out?

1878 WYR get lost in the pages of a book for four hours or lose four hours on Facebook?

1879 WYR never steal a robe from a hotel or never steal a kiss from someone who is in a relationship?

1880 WYR save someone from drowning or save a goal in soccer so your team wins?

1881 WYR be stranded in a desert with just a pocketknife or stranded in a jungle with only a rope?

1882 WYR be trapped in an underwater cave with only thirty seconds of air or three hours of air and no hope of rescue?

1883 WYR try to escape from the Temple of Doom with Indiana Jones or escape from the KGB with James Bond?

1884 WYR be the only person in town who doesn't have a car or the only person in town who does have a car?

1885 WYR have Mary Poppins's magic carpet bag or flying umbrella?

1886 WYR count your steps out loud as you walk or count backwards from ten before going through any door?

1887 WYR be able to travel through time or through dimensions?

1888 WYR be assimilated by the Borg or attacked by the Death Star?

1889 WYR be frugal or stubborn?

1890 WYR live in an Amish community for a week or go on a Buddhist retreat for a week?

1891 WYR follow a will-o'-the-wisp or stay on the beaten path?

1892 WYR your hair never tangled or your feet never got cheesy?

1893 WYR work twelve-hour shifts for three days each week or work offshore for three weeks and have three weeks off?

1894 WYR be an old lady's cat or the Hello Kitty cat?

1895 WYR see imaginary spiders or feel imaginary spiders?

1896 WYR scream out loud in a movie theater or ugly cry in a movie theater?

1897 WYR your parents never cried happy tears or your children never cried sad tears?

1898 WYR never fire a gun or never be mugged?

1899 WYR create a punishment for people who take all the red Skittles or people who leave an empty toilet roll holder?

1900 WYR have a huge imagination or a photographic memory?

1901 WYR have a full body wax or wax five cars by hand?

1902 WYR push over someone's snowman or step on someone's sandcastle?

1903 WYR get rid of one bad habit or gain one new good habit?

1904 WYR have actual butterfingers or actual fish fingers?

1905 WYR have 330 people at your family reunion or thirty-three?

1906 WYR sleepwalk or sleep talk?

1907 WYR date someone with the same name as one of your siblings or the same name as your dog?

1908 WYR be named after a color or a virtue?

1909 WYR earn someone's respect or earn someone's gratitude?

1910 WYR end all illegal animal trading or have your favorite animal become extinct?

1911 WYR binge-watch TV all day or binge on junk food all day?

1912 WYR have a strong opinion or sit on the fence?

1913 WYR knock over the first domino in someone's long line or knock down someone's house of cards?

1914 WYR not be able to use a corkscrew or a can opener?

1915 WYR never have another bad thought or never get invited to another good party?

1916 WYR be considered "gifted" or "special"?

1917 WYR be hypercritical or a hypocrite?

1918 WYR be half-human, half-fly or a reverse mermaid (merman)?

1919 WYR be someone to rely on or be reliably unreliable?

1920 WYR never bite off more than you can chew or never bite the hand that feeds?

1921 WYR face the Spanish Inquisition or "The Wrath of Khan"?

1922 WYR not be able to open any closed doors or not be able to close any open doors?

1923 WYR compromise on where you live or where you go on vacation?

1924 WYR dress as a Viking or as a Marvel character for a day?

1925 WYR have an actual sheepdog (sheep mixed with dog) or an actual bird dog (bird mixed with dog)?

1926 WYR see a bunny that can jive or a chicken that can dance?

1927 WYR be true to your zodiac sign or your Chinese zodiac animal?

1928 WYR be an expert calligrapher or an expert bingo caller?

1929 WYR hold a grudge or hold the record for "the most sticky notes on the face in one minute"?

1930 WYR be someone who gets the ball rolling or someone who can roll with the punches?

1931 WYR be impressive or be an impressionist?

1932 WYR have your face slammed into a cake or have a door slammed in your face?

1933 WYR put your finger into a yawning dog's mouth or kiss a duck?

1934 WYR ride on the roof of a car or ride in a supermarket shopping cart?

1935 WYR eat food in a supermarket before paying for it or crash a wedding party?

1936 WYR pee outdoors or pee in the sink?

1937 WYR dress up as a robber with a stocking on your head or as a bandit with a dish towel as a poncho?

1938 WYR eat a brilliant meal in a bad restaurant or an awful meal in an amazing restaurant?

1939 WYR dress in a single color or always wear a hat?

1940 WYR put something on the stove and forget about it or fall asleep in the sun and get burned?

1941 WYR get your tongue pierced or be a nude life model in an art class?

1942 WYR drive a limousine or drive a hard bargain?

1943 WYR be seated next to a dog or a chicken on a plane?

1944 WYR have extrasensory abilities or be able to jump rope effortlessly for fifteen minutes?

1945 WYR have a partner who snores in bed or talks in their sleep?

1946 WYR be a fast talker or a slow eater?

1947 WYR let it go or fight tooth and nail to hold on to it?

1948 WYR know the true meaning of freedom or the true meaning of peace?

1949 WYR give up your most prized possession or give up a $100,000 prize?

1950 WYR never doubt yourself or never do anything spontaneous?

1951 WYR enjoy simple pleasures or strive to experience the finer things in life?

1952 WYR never tell a white lie or never see red?

1953 WYR have someone to watch over you or watch the world go by with friends?

1954 WYR hit the dance floor or hit the hay?

1955 WYR accidentally break a window or spill ketchup on your friend's white top?

1956 WYR share food with your dog or share your bed with a cat?

1957 WYR be able to talk your way out of trouble or be a guest on a talk show?

1958 WYR be someone who can't hit the broad side of a barn or someone who is prone to hitting the roof?

1959 WYR have an attic full of things to remind you of your past or just one photograph?

1960 WYR grow old gracefully or be the oldest swinger in town?

1961 WYR fall on hard times or fall from grace?

1962 WYR lie about your likes and dislikes on a date or lie about your experience in a job interview?

1963 WYR never be depressed or never have to eat humble pie?

1964 WYR play hardball or play hard to get?

1965 WYR not care what you wear or not care about what others think of you?

1966 WYR only be able to eat cold food for the rest of your life or only be able to take cold showers?

1967 WYR have sand in your underpants or honey in your footwear?

1968 WYR have everything you drop be gone forever or be unable to say goodbye to workmates every day without crying?

1969 WYR have your eyes stay closed for five seconds whenever you blink or your mouth stay open for five minutes when you yawn?

1970 WYR burst into tears or burst into song whenever you're hungry?

1971 WYR hear a buzzer every time something touches your lips or make a beeping sound when you chew?

1972 WYR be trapped in a room full of spiders or one filled with snakes?

1973 WYR be unable to make any facial expressions or start drooling whenever you see someone you like?

1974 WYR have your shoelaces tied together or wear a watermelon helmet?

1975 WYR babies cry when you look at them or dogs howl when you go near them?

1976 WYR go upstairs on your hands and knees or go downstairs on your butt?

1977 WYR chug everything you drink or have your mouth stay open all day?

1978 WYR create a punishment for people who jump lines or people who shout into their phones?

1979 WYR wake up with an upside-down face or with your arms and legs attached backwards?

1980 WYR go to work on a hippity-hop or by jumping in a sack?

1981 WYR get an electric shock every time you receive a text message or every time you touch someone?

1982 WYR spend a day with everything in life moving in slow motion or a day when you do everything twice as fast?

1983 WYR get a one-off one minute of free shopping in a store of your choice or a personal assistant for a week?

1984 WYR feel compelled to yell "Shark!" whenever you swim in the sea or "Stick 'em up!" whenever you go into a bank?

1985 WYR lose your internet connection whenever you open the fridge door or have the fuses blow every time you sneeze?

1986 WYR develop an irrational fear of trash cans or be afraid of your own shadow?

1987 WYR have the music stop whenever you get up to dance or have a fly go in your mouth every time you yawn?

1988 WYR carry a rose between your teeth or burp loudly whenever you speak?

1989 WYR be able to remember everything in every book you read or remember every conversation you have?

1990 WYR wake up every morning with a new $100 bill in your pocket but not know where it came from or wake up every morning with a new $50 bill in your pocket and know where it came from?

1991 WYR everyone always laughed at your jokes or you received at least one compliment every day?

1992 WYR be able to take pictures by blinking your eyes or memorize words by running your finger over them?

1993 WYR not be able to use (speak or write) the letter "w" or have everything you say repeated back to you?

1994 WYR have a small snail living in your ear or a small worm living in your nose?

1995 WYR not shower for a week or not brush your teeth for a week?

1996 WYR take one step back after every two steps forward or clap your hands in time with every step you take?

1997 WYR narrate everything you do or carry your partner on your back?

1998 WYR grow a tail or an extra leg?

1999 WYR be able to teleport or own a clone of yourself?

2000 WYR marry for love or money?

About Us

We're an odd bunch of fun, quirky, and creative authors who love writing thought-provoking questions. And we're on a mission to spark engaging discussions.

We've all experienced awkward silence situations and resorted to superficial chitchat and small talk to pass time.

The authors here at *Questions About Me* are on a mission to end dull conversations. We created the *Questions About Me* series to invigorate conversations and help you get to know people better – including yourself.

Put down your phone, switch off the TV, and use our *Questions About Me* books to unlock endless conversational possibilities, provide an abundance of fun memories, and develop deeper relationships.

www.questionsaboutme.com

Also by Questions About Me

3000 Unique Questions About Me

2000 Unique Questions About Me

1000 Unique Questions About Me

Printed in Great Britain
by Amazon

28491513R00065